"I am not the only IRS employee who's wondered why churches go to the government and seek permission to be exempted from a tax they didn't owe to begin with, and to seek a tax deductible status that they've always had anyway. Many of us have marveled at how church leaders want to be regulated and controlled by an agency of government that most Americans have prayed would just get out of their lives. Churches are in an amazingly unique position, but they don't seem to know or appreciate the implications of what it would mean to be free of government control."

Steve Nestor, Senior IRS Agent (Ret), from the Forward of *In Caesar's Grip*, by Peter Kershaw

The Corporation Sole
Freeing America's Pulpits and ENDING the Restrictive 501c3 Laws for Churches

For 24/7 Support, Please visit:
www.ChurchFreedom.org/support

Authored By,
The Empowerment Center Overseer and Successors, a Corporation Sole.

For the Instruction and preparation of ministers.

This book or parts thereof may not be reproduced in any form, stored in a retrieval system, or transmitted in any form by any means – electronic, mechanical, photocopy, recording, or otherwise – without prior written permission by the author, except as provided by United States of America copyright law.

Unless otherwise noted, all scripture quotations are from the New International Version of the Bible.

Cover Design by Terrence Lester of U-Turn Books, LLC.

Copyright © 2013 by The Empowerment Center Overseer and Successors, a Corporation Sole.

LEGAL DISCLAIMER - THIS IS MINISTRY ADVICE NOT LEGAL ADVICE. I am just a fellow brother in the Lord with a vision to help raise up the next generation of leaders for the body of Christ. I am neither an Attorney nor a Certified Public Accountant. Make sure you always do your own due diligence and contact an attorney or CPA regarding any legal matters.

- Dedications -

This book is dedicated to my wife Mandy for inspiring me to write this. She has taught me through Christ the true meaning of how to have unlimited love. She is the epitome of every single quality a man could hope for in a noble Godly wife. For my son Jacob Alexander and his incredible diligence, trustworthiness and faithfulness to this family, for my son Justin David for his sense of wonder and humor that makes all of us smile each day, for my daughter Faith Victoria for stealing my heart and breaking all boundaries with having a heart of joy, for my earthly father Robert Greenwood for his steadfast faithfulness to me and my family during great times of hardship and believing in the spirit of the Lord that was upon me when so many turned away. To Pastor Brandi Stephens and her absolutely incredible heart supernatural faith and love. Supernatural faith in even the most incredibly difficult of circumstances. For Apostle Ron Carpenter Jr. and Redemption World Outreach Center for teaching me such a wealth of biblical knowledge and understanding. To Overseer Thomas Clark for believing in me and opening the doors to his Church to us when so many would turn their backs to me and to ALL those nameless brothers and sisters in Christ that will heed the call of this book and bring forth Godly order back to the church. May the Lord give us all providence and peace in this coming hour.

IMPORTANT NOTICE: I wanted the reader to be given nothing but TRUTH, FACT and EVIDENCE related to the Corporation Sole and how to FREE America's churches from government rule. Everything in this book can be fact checked and easily verified by the reader as completely accurate.

"A gift opens the way and ushers the giver into the presence of the great." **- Proverbs 18:16**

Table of Contents

- **Chapter 1: Our Vision and the Problem Facing Today's Churches**..15

- **Chapter 2 - History of the Corporation Sole and Modern Day Taxation in the United States**...................22

- **Chapter 3 – THE CHURCH ESTABLISHMENT AFFIDAVIT and WHY it is so vital to your Church/Ministry and Corporation Sole**......................27

- **Chapter 4 – Easy Instructions for How to Quickly Set Up Both Your Church and It's Subsequent Corporation Sole**..37

    1. Step #1 Modify, Sign, Witness and have Notarized Your Official Church Establishment Affidavit............37
    2. Step #2 Get a Registered Agent..............................38
    3. Step #3 Get your Corporation Sole's EIN number, Bank Accounts and Subsequent Tax Exempted PayPal Account (for receiving donations online)...................39
    4. SET UP YOUR CORPORATION SOLE'S TAX EXEMPTED PAYPAL ACCOUNT...40

- **Chapter 5 – Legal Facts, Questions and Answers Related to the Corporation Sole**...........Begins on Page 43

Contains Questions Such As:
1. What are the 7 States that still have active Corporation Sole laws?...43
2. What if there are church members in a different state, can they still sign our affidavit?...43
3. What are common mistakes churches make when establishing themselves, mistakes that erroneously place them under the jurisdiction of 501c3?................................43
4. Can a church reorganize its current 501c3 status in favor

of a Corporation Sole?..50
5. If I get a Corporation Sole, will my church be considered a 501c3?..52
6. If our church decides to reorganize with a Corporate Sole, can our church be actively involved in political propaganda, attempt to influence legislation or publish political statements on behalf of (or in opposition to) any candidate for public office?...53
7. What is the difference or advantages of the Corporation Sole versus a traditional 501c3?...55
8. Can our church have a Corporate Sole even if we do not live in one of the 7 States that has Corporate Sole Laws?..57
9. Do you need to have a physical church building (i.e. 4 walls and a steeple) in order to have a Corporation Sole?...58
10. Is a Corporation Sole lawfully required to have a polity body or board of trustees like other 501c3's?.........................59
11. Do you need to become an ordained minister in order to form a Corporation Sole?..59
12. Is the Corporate Sole a scam?..60
13. Can you have a church located in one state yet have a Corporation Sole organized in another state?.......................61
14. What qualifications should you have before getting a Corporation Sole?..62
15. How much does it cost to incorporate a Corporation Sole?...63
16. Does the Corporate Sole need to have the name of the church in its incorporated name?...63
17. Will the Corporation Sole's incorporated name affect the way people can write tax-deductible checks to your church and or ministry?...64
18. What if we have many subsidiaries to our ministry (*such as an outreach center*) that we would like to collect separate donations for? Will donors still be able to donate to those various ministries?..64
19. Is a Corporation Sole required by Federal Law to file annual information returns?...65

20. Is property held by a Corporate Sole considered tax exempt?..66
21. If I am personally blessed with a large cash tithe of offering or any offering for that matter, can I give it to the Corporate Sole and claim it as a deduction?........................67
22. What about non-cash contributions of property(s) to the Corporation Sole?..67
    **In this section, we explain in detail:*
    - *1. Fair market value of contributed property*
    - *2. What about non-cash contributions totaling more than $500?*
    - *3. Regarding car contributions: You MUST have written acknowledgement.*
    - *4. Non-cash contributions over $5,000: You must have written appraisal.*
    - *5. Limits on the charitable contribution deduction*
    - *6. Non-tax deductible items to consider for the Corporation Sole.*
23. Is my church required to have a Federal Tax EIN number or ANY Federal Tax Identification number?......................69
24. Is the Corporate Sole required to have an EIN?...................69
25. If the Corporate Sole is exempted from taxation, how does our church keep up with its bookkeeping?.........................70
26. Is the Corporate Sole required to receive its tax exempt status from the IRS?..70
27. Can a Corporate Sole open up a bank account or an online merchant account (such as a PayPal account)?...................70
28. How does the law define a church?..70
29. Can an individual, unbeliever or person of a different faith set up a Corporation Sole?..71
30. Can a Corporation Sole receive grants?................................71
31. Can a Corporation Sole own a business?..............................72
32. Does a Corporation Sole receive discounts on postage like other non-profits?...73
33. How do I know if my church is a 501c3?................................73
34. Does the Government have jurisdiction over my Corporate Sole and, what are some legal advantages of the Corporation Sole?..74

35. What if our church applies for a Corporation Sole in one of the 7 States, and then that state repeals their Corporation Sole law? What happens to our Corporation Sole if or when that happens?...................75
36. Does the Corporation Sole get filed like any other corporation through the Secretary of State?...................76
37. Does the Church Establishment Affidavit get filed through the Secretary of State?...................76
38. When should we open up our Corporation Sole's checking or savings accounts?...................76
39. Am I required to take a, "Vow of Poverty", when setting up a church or a Corporation Sole?...................76
40. How long does it take from start to finish to completely and totally set up a Corporation Sole (from initial application to opening up all subsequent bank accounts and even PayPal accounts)?...................80
41. Should a checking account be established before any tithes, offerings or donations are received? Can a donor just write a donation check out to me personally until I set up the church's bank accounts?...................80
42. *Are both a church and its subsequent Corporation Sole required to have by-laws?*...................81
43. Can the Corporation Sole's Successor and Secretary be the same person or two different people? Can either my underage son or daughter be named to either of these positions as well?...................83
44. Can an individual person have multiple Corporation Soles?...................83
45. The introduction of IRS publication 1827 States: "Churches and religious organizations may be legally organized in a variety of ways under state law, such as unincorporated associations, nonprofit corporations, corporations sole, and charitable trusts." Isn't a church that is legally established under any of these organizations subject to the 26 U.S.C § 508(c)(1)(a) exemption law?...................84
46. How does a Corporation Sole protect a church any differently from all 501c3 stipulations (such as political

lobbying)? It seems to be that the Church, (no matter how it is legally formed), is still subject to all qualifications and disqualifications of the 501c3 law..84
47. CALIFORNIA Corporation Sole regulation (10009) stipulates that "Any judge of the superior court in the county in which a corporation sole has its principal office shall at all times have access to the books of the corporation." If I establish a Corporation Sole through another state, but still have my principal office in California, aren't my books still accessible by the Superior Court in the county where my principal office is?..85
48. If I am not trying to hide behind a "tax shelter" or get out of paying "unrelated business entity taxes" then why should it matter if my books are available to a Superior Court – IF both myself, my members and contributors have followed the stipulations regarding "donations and contributions" outlined for Corporations by the Secretary of State and by the IRS tax codes sections 501-508?..85
49. What's the legal definition of a Corporation Sole?............86
50. When signing legal documents on behalf of my ministry's Corporation Sole, do I need to use my personal signature or sign in the name of the Corporation Sole itself?...........86
51. Can a Corporation Sole issue Promissory Notes?.............86
52. Since Christians are the Temple of the Holy Ghost, would that not make us automatically tax exempt at our conversion and confirmed by our baptismal record?..87
53. Is the Corporation Sole Considered Either a Church or a Ministry?..87
54. Is there a reason why the ALL CAPS names are used when signing our Church Affidavit? Doesn't that name in ALL CAPITAL LETTERS signify the Government created, "Strawman"?..87
55. Does the Corporation Sole receive a Tax Exempt ID number from the IRS?..89

56. Can a Corporation Sole Issue a Receipt for any Tithe or Donation that a donor can use for tax write-off?................89
57. Our church takes in voluntary contributions on a monthly basis of less than $500 a month, the fact that our monthly voluntary contributions intake is so minimal, in your opinion is it just as imperative and advantageous to take the steps necessary to terminate our 501c(3) and move into a corporation sole?................90
58. Would like to understand better how a corporation sole can use three separate individuals in its governing structure. I understand that your incorporating an office and let's say the lead minister holds that office, can you still have a separate individual NOT related to you, as a secretary, even a third individual as an additional director if we choose to do so?................91
59. How to obtain an EIN for a Corporation Sole?................91
60. Can a Corporation Sole Issue a Receipt for any Tithe or Donation that a donor can use for tax write-off?................92
61. If I was the overseer and my spouse as the successor and secretary pass away who will then own the church and the corporation sole?................92
62. Is there an age requirement for opening a corporation sole? I have a son or daughter that is in their twenties...93
63. Describe the IRS and Courts 14 Point Test and How does the Affidavit lawfully fulfill these points?................93
64. We already have an EIN number because we established a checking account. We have it in one city but about to plant the church in another city. Would we just give the state a change of address for the EIN number, how does that work?................94
65. With the states trying to do away with Corporate Soles, what is the status of Oregon State. Since in Missouri we would have to go through you, therefore if Oregon followed suit would we lose it or would we be grandfathered in it. With the states trying to do away with Corporate Soles, what is the status of Oregon State. Since in Missouri we would have to go through you, therefore if

Oregon followed suit would we lose it or would we be grandfathered in it..95
66. Does a Minister that has a Corporation Sole give themselves a Ministers Stipend Salary AND Do we pay personal income tax for any income received from the Corporation Sole?...95
67. How Would I as a Senior Pastor to Our Church Compute Self-Employment Tax if we do not apply or seek a Self Employment Tax Exemptions..................................98
68. Should a Church pay its staff an Employee's or Independent Contractors?...100
69. What Income Should Be Reported to the IRS as Income Generated from Either the Church or The Corporation Sole?..104
    a.) Income Issues...105
    b.) Income To Be Reported................................105
    c.) Gift or Compensation for Services.............106
    d.) The Parsonage Allowance............................108
    e.) Retired Ministers...113
    f.) Members of Religious Orders and Vow of Poverty..113

- **Chapter 6 - What should I do if our church or Corporation Sole are ever presented with a certified letter notice from the IRS for either a formal IRS audit, intent to levy or a formal church Inquiry?**..117

- **CHAPTER 7 – As an Overseer or Bishop, I would like to ordain ministers underneath our covering of ministry, am I able to do this with a Corporation Sole?**..133
  Includes:
  - *ASSOCIATION CHURCH AND ORDINATION AFFIDAVIT*
  - *1st AMENDMENT TO THE ASSOCIATION CHURCH AND ORDINATION AFFIDAVIT - Detailing both the Successor and Secretary of the Association Church's Corporation Sole.*

- **Chapter 8 – Call to Action!**...151

- **Chapter 9 – Church Establishment Affidavit (Now includes language that lawfully fulfills the IRS's own 14 Points to a church!)**......................................152
PRESCRIBED 1ˢᵗ Amendment, detailing the position of "Overseer"..165
PRESCRIBED 2ⁿᵈ Amendment, detailing the position of both the Successor and Secretary of your Church's Corporation Sole...173
Contact Joshua or The Empowerment Center................177
Notes...178

Pastoral Reviews and Endorsements..............................179

About Overseer Joshua Kenny-Greenwood.......................186

Chapter 1: Our Vision and the Problem Facing Today's Churches:

"The Only Thing Necessary for the Triumph of Evil is for Good Men to do nothing."
-Edmund Burke

Our Vision Statement for This Book:

Our vision is bold, Holy Spirit inspired and very simple: To help raise up the next generation of leaders for the Body of Christ and to help set America's churches FREE from the control and restrictions of 501c3. It is our sincere desire that you as the reader of this material help us in getting this book into the hands of every church pastor here in America.

I should also note that this book represents the accumulation of thousands of hours of painstaking research. After helping churches and Corporation Sole's across America, after reviewing nearly ALL available information regarding the IRS successfully prosecuting BOTH churches and Corporation Soles, after hours of recorded consultations with BOTH the US Department of Justice and the Internal Revenue Service, after reviewing nearly ALL State and Federal Laws related to churches, this book gives the reader answers to nearly EVERY conceivable question one would have if they were interested in either planting a new church or reorganizing their present church to be out from underneath the manipulative laws of 501c3. With the reader keeping in mind that the topic of the Corporation Sole has not been taught in ANY seminary, theology, or in any law schools here in the United States of America.

In addition, I have purposefully left out a vast majority of my personal philosophical views (to which, I could have written another 500+ pages of content). I felt that the majority of the readers of this material (like yourself reading this now) are being called to be the next generation of leaders the Body of Christ needs. There is a quickening in my spirit that *time is of the essence*. It is critical to begin equipping the saints for the time of great calamity that is soon coming upon us. It is time to restore Godly order to both the church and to creation itself.

It's time to confront the spirit of fear that prevents a pastor from preaching against abortion or the same fear that silences a prophet from speaking out against a political candidate for public office who they know to have a heart of ungodliness. To stop the manipulative fear that paralyzes a teacher from telling their congregation that marriage is for life and that divorce was never intended to be an option, and the same fear that pressures an apostle to never attempt to openly influence or promote righteous legislation to bring creation itself back into its glorious freedom of Godly order.

We have been called to rule this Earth and told that we're more than conquerors. Our position in the Lord is so significant, that it is proclaimed in 1st Corinthians 6:3, *"Do you not know that we will judge angels? How much more the things of this life!"* and that according to Romans 8:20-21, *"For the creation was subjected to frustration, not by its own choice, but by the will of the one who subjected it, in hope that the creation itself will be liberated from its bondage to decay and brought into the freedom and glory of the children of God."* This means God deliberately brought frustration to ALL of creation (the Universe itself) in hopes that WE as the children of God will use our anointed gifts and talents to bring forth Godly order, in hopes to liberate the creation and bring it into both freedom and glory!

 Do you know who you are and who the God is that you serve?

Yet, if we're so powerful, why do we have a Christian divorce rate of nearly 60%? Why are our homes being split up? Why are so many of our children without fathers? Why are our children not being taught that marriage is for life and divorce is not even an option for consideration? Why instead of complaining about homosexual television programming like NBC's, "The New Normal" are we not instead "buying" NBC and creating our own programs? Instead of complaining about banks and foreclosures, why are we not instead "becoming banks"?

Why? I'll tell you why, it's because since 1969 we have had nearly 4 generations of Christian leaders that have completely disenfranchised the Body of Christ. By our very definition as leaders, we are supposed to be teachers of the law and yet 90% of the pastors I speak with can't even tell me the difference between 501c3 and 508c1a of our own US Code of Laws! If they can't explain to me modern law, how in the world are they going to teach the Body of Christ Biblical law?! This gives new meaning to when the Apostle Paul wrote in 1st Timothy 1:7-8 which states, *"They want to be teachers of the law, but they do not know what they are talking about or what they so confidently affirm! But we know the Law is good when one teaches it properly,..."*

How can anyone honestly understand where his or her grace comes from without first being taught the law?! Without the law, grace has no meaning!

Therefore, this is for those brothers and sisters that will heed the call of this book, who never had the knowledge in how to properly organize their ministry or calling. This book is PURE KNOWLEDGE. It is the "how to" and "trade secrets" that will empower you to take your ministry to its next level. Take this incredible gift of knowledge and go forth to bring freedom BACK to The Body of Christ!

The Problem Facing Today's Churches:

Exodus 9:1 says, *"Then the LORD said to Moses, "Go in to Pharaoh and say to him, 'Thus says the LORD, the God of the Hebrews, "Let my people go, that they may serve me."*

My fellow Christians, the Body of Christ is in bondage! Just like the Hebrews of old that were servants under the Pharaoh, the Federal Law of 501c3 has effectively enslaved the modern day church and the Body of Christ.

There was no other reason for President Lyndon Johnson to draft 501c3 into law other than for the intent of silencing the church in all matters of Government. This was its intended purpose and now after only 44 short years, it has all but accomplished its task. The law of 501c3 has created a crisis of such epic proportions since 1969, in only a few short generations since the passage of that law by President Lyndon Johnson, so that currently today 100% of registered or incorporated churches in the United States are now lawfully considered to be "Creatures of the State"!

100% of these 501c3 churches are legally and contractually obligated to adhere to the severe restrictions of 501c3 in order to claim the "*conditional privilege*" of tax exemption. If you're a ministry leader reading this and you're under the false impression that you're in fact NOT under 501c3's jurisdiction simply because you did not apply for 'recognition' of your 501c3 status, then go ahead this Sunday morning and simultaneously video record and tell your congregation members that you would like for them to vote for or against a political candidate for office! Tell them to pass out brochures to their community in an effort to directly influence political legislation and then tell them that your church plans on lobbying Congress. Record the entire church service and then send that recording as a formal complaint to the IRS commissioner in your local jurisdiction and then find out within 30 days what happens to your church's tax-exempt status! You see, if your church has either an incorporation, bank account, financial trust or ANY financial mechanism in place to receive tax deductible contributions and your church does NOT have a Corporation Sole, then your church is 100% completely underneath the entire jurisdiction of the 501c3 law. So, do not be fooled by these "free-church" enthusiasts out there that claim to be able to help churches establish non-501c3, "ministerial trusts" or 508 Church Trusts. Such trusts have absolutely no merit whatsoever in law that exempts you from the jurisdiction of the 501c3 law. In fact, these trusts peddled by "free-church" advocates can in fact get your church in more trouble because they are set up so improperly.

Brothers and sisters in Christ, this book will explain in detail why never before has it been more imperative that the church come out from underneath the control of the government and be placed BACK under the headship of our Lord and Savior Jesus Christ. With such critical governmental and social issues ranging from eternal salvation, marriage, divorce, teen pregnancy, privacy right violations, civil rights, taxation, abortion, GMO foods, enforced vaccinations, parent religious exemption rights, gay marriage, homosexual, transgendered and bi-sexual rights, etc., it's never been more important than ever for leadership and the entire church to come together and speak out. To organize and lead voters to directly influence legislation related to these matters. Many of these government policies (such as the recently revealed National Security Agency's data gathering program) pose a direct threat to the church! Imagine if such an incredible data collection tool was placed into the hands of the Antichrist! Or if both state and federal governments try to redefine the definition of marriage when they had no jurisdiction over it in the first place because such jurisdiction belongs to the church and the church alone, as originally specified in God's word.

In fact on Saturday, March 7th, 2015 at 10:12am PST (confirmed with time date stamps online that cannot be altered), I was led by the Holy Spirit to write an email to 10,000+ Pastors in which the Spirit of The Lord said,

"Did you hear that our President just fully endorsed nationwide gay marriage? Remember when we told you that the IRS would come after Churches and it did? Remember when we told that the LGBT community would begin suing Churches for discrimination and it happened? Or when the state would force Churches to get "business licenses" and no one wanted to listen?

So that you continue to know that there are still prophets among you that speak from his power and authority, understand in advance that the US Supreme court is going to rule in favor of Gay marriage. Understand this was given to you in advance so that you know before it takes place what would happen! REMEMBER THIS! Remember these words you saints that had any doubt. Remember when God gave the Church the opportunity to freely remove themselves from this legal nightmare and the restrictions the Government imposes on Churches with the help of the Church Establishment Affidavit and the Corporation Sole! Pray that the doors don't close too fast when the enemy realizes the tactical mistake it made by forgetting the Corporation Sole existed! Pray that the day doesn't come when your Church wakes up and wants to get this freedom but can no longer do so because they changed the laws (because it will happen)! "

On June 26, 2015 this prophetic word was fulfilled and the United States Supreme Court has redefined and fully endorsed gay marriage. Now, those Churches that do not have a Church Establishment Affidavit and Corporation Sole will be legally forced under Federal, State and Local "Gender Discrimination Laws" to accept gay marriage or have their Churches tax exemptions revoked or worse, like in Idaho, they now threaten Pastors with jail time for not accepting gay marriage! Only those Churches that have their Church Establishment Affidavits and Corporation Soles will be lawfully immune to these Gender Discrimination laws.

These reasons are WHY this book is so important to place into the hands of each pastor here in America! Because Corporation Sole is the only known lawful way a church can organize its financial assets, whereas the church itself is NOT considered to be under the law of 501c3 but instead under the jurisdiction of both 26 U.S.C § 508(c)(1)(a) and 26 U.S.C § 6033(3)(a)(1-3).

To understand this better, please allow me to briefly explain the aspects of both the history of the Corporation Sole as well as the modern 501c3 law here in the United States and WHY the Corporation Sole is the saving grace for the church.

- Churches are forced to have business licenses

CANON LAW = Church Law

Chapter 2 - History of the Corporation Sole and Modern Taxation in the United States:

The Corporation Sole is one of the oldest forms of a Corporation in the world. The initial genesis of the Corporation Sole dates back to Roman Emperor Constantine in the year 323 AD (After Constantine declared Christianity the official religion of the Roman Empire). The Pope first used the Corporation Sole for use by the Bishops of the church for ecclesiastical purposes and, in particular, holding church property and other assets. The Bishop was authorized to act on his own authority, absent the control of a typical board of directors.

When the Bishop resigned his position, died, was incapacitated, or was forcefully removed from office by the presiding pope or archbishop, then title to the property passed not to the bishop's heirs (even though Catholic bishops were not permitted to marry, it was not uncommon that they had several children), but to a successor that is designated by the corporate sole (usually another bishop). While the office of corporate sole held title to property, that property did not "belong" to the bishop personally. Rather, he held the property in trust for the church. In this sense, the bishop was very much like a trustee. Those ancient Corporation Soles were often formed under canon law (church law) and, therefore, absent the permission and jurisdiction of the state.

The use of the ecclesiastical Corporation Sole by Catholic bishops and leaders continued largely uninterrupted for a number of centuries. However, things began to radically change in the sixteenth century, regarding the fundamental nature and legal attributes of the Corporation Sole. This was largely the result of an historic phenomenon known today as "The Reformation". The Reformation spread like wildfire throughout a number of European nations. Due to the nature of this question, I will focus attention on England and the significance of its actions in relationship to the modern day Corporation Sole.

- TAX LAW
- The Church of England

In 1534, King Henry VIII split from the church in an act of rebellion that is known today as, "The Act of Supremacy". The motives behind this split were due to King Henry VIII having an affair and wanting to divorce his current wife. Because the Catholic Church was solely in charge of any potential dissolutions of marriage, King Henry VIII sought the Pope's approval for being able to marry his mistress. The Pope denied this request, which greatly angered the King. In essence, what transpired next was the formation of one of the world's first denominational splits. The King decided to forgo the "divine right of popes" in favor of his new doctrine of "the divine right of kings" and thus crowned himself the "lord sovereign head" of the Church of England. It was also at this time that the Church of England became Anglican (Episcopal). At this time the Church-State was effectively replaced by a State-Church. *Which on a side note, if you think about why the Anglican church today has openly homosexual bishops, it's rooted in the fact that the genesis of this church was created from the desires of a sexually deviant king!* When the head is out of order, the whole body is out of order!

From this point, much of the Church of England was reformed. For example, adoration of Mary (Mariolatry) and prayer to the saints was abolished as idolatrous. Their various statues were declared "idols" and were removed from all church properties. Worship of the elements of the Eucharist was declared to be idolatry. Transubstantiation was deemed heresy. Reciting the rosary on rosary beads was deemed "vain pagan repetition". In addition, the Latin Mass was declared superstitious and was abolished in favor of an English worship service which emphasized the preaching of God's Word *(in a language the people could understand, because up until this point, the word of God was being preached in Latin).*

As a means of controlling the people, and keeping them subservient to Catholic leadership hierarchy, the Roman Catholic Church had, for many centuries, prevented the people from knowing what the Word of God says and reading it themselves. The Reformation forever abolished this. The Word of God was

Episcopal = Bishop Rule

translated into the common tongue and eagerly given to the people. The English Bible translator, William Tyndale, foretold that, *"every plowboy would read the Scripture for himself"*.

But for many, the Reformation was also not as thoroughgoing as they had hoped for. Certain vestiges of Roman Catholicism remained, including the office of corporate sole. However, with the Act of Supremacy, and the king being declared the "lord sovereign head of the church", there also began to emerge a new understanding of who (or what) was head of the Corporation Sole. In this State-Church system the Corporation Sole was promptly converted into a creature of civil law. Bishops, rather than being emissaries of the pope, were now agents of the king and of the state.

Since the Anglican Church of England was (and is) a hierarchical church governed from the top down by bishops ("episcopal" meaning "bishop rule"), and since members in such a church have little if any say in the governance of their church, the office of the corporate sole was inherently consonant with the church structure in England.

However, nearer to the 1700's, attitudes in the American Colonies about church polity were altogether different. Rather than a top-down bishop-rule hierarchy, most Colonial American churches were governed bottom-up, usually by elders elected by the local congregation, and such elders were always accountable to those who had elected them. Accountability was the key to preventing the potential tyrannies of bishops endemic in both Catholicism and Anglicanism.

As the Rev. Cotton Mather put it: *"Never entrust a man with more power than you are content for him to use; for use it he will."* A great many of the Colonists had known first-hand the abuses of the English Bishopric, as exercised through the office of corporate sole. Star Chamber abuses, or "examinations", under torture, including widespread executions at the hands of the bishops, had become a major factor in "religious nonconformists" coming to America.

Ultimately, the Corporation Sole did find its way to America by way of England. However, the Corporation Sole never gained recognition in the American Colonies as a canon law institution. In fact, it's impossible to identify any specific historic example of the use of the canon law Corporation Sole in America, either before or after America gained independence, whether by Catholics or anyone else. Catholic scholars deny that the Corporation Sole, as used in America, has ever been anything other than a civil law entity.

Because the Corporation Sole was so rarely used by the early colonists and states, there are almost no records of its existence in many states historical records. In fact, it is so rare that currently, no state east of the Mississippi even has a Corporation Sole law (*even in the Bible belt of America*)! Because of its rarity here in America, it is currently not taught about in ANY known seminary school, theological university, or law school here in the United States of America. Not a single minister we've spoken with (which have been thousands) has even heard of its existence when getting their ordination licenses.

Right now, since 1969, the United States government has done everything within its power to silence the modern day Body of Christ from all matters of politics. The genesis of the law of 501c3 actually came as a direct result of the church standing up during the civil rights movements of the 1960's. In 1964 and 1968, church leaders all over America stood in solidarity against segregation. Leaders such as Reverend Dr. Martin Luther King Jr. were instrumental in forming what we know today as, "The Civil Rights Act of 1964 and 1968." The government (*specifically then Senator Lyndon B. Johnson*) fearing the power of the church to influence legislation and politics, immediately began drafting the 501c3 law into existence. In October 9th, 1969 the 501c3 was written and signed into law by then Senator and eventually President Lyndon B. Johnson.

501(c)(1)(a)

It also needs to be historically relevant to note that President Johnson was known as a man that exhibited both fear and manipulation. Many historians nicknamed his manipulation tactic "The Johnson Treatment". His Presidency was also considered at that time as the height of modern day liberalism here in America. Is it any wonder that 501c3 creates such fear and manipulation in churches? It's law was written by a man that did nothing but promote fear and manipulation!

I have a quote on the first page of my prayer journal from Edmund Burke that declares, *"The only thing necessary for the triumph of evil, is for good men to do nothing."*

Presently, Christians account for more then 70% of registered voters. If churches reorganize their financial structures to a Corporation Sole and thus bring the entirety of their ministry out from underneath the manipulative 'conditional privilege' of tax-exemption under the law of 501c3 and instead brought the church under both 26 § 508(c)(1)(a) and 26 U.S.C § 6033(3)(a)(1-3) - which contain NO conditions to the privilege of tax exemption - then we would experience a gigantic "Kingdom Shift" in this country. The Internal Revenue Service would leave the church alone. Policy makers would be treating the church as the most significant voter base in America and would be begging us for political favor. Laws such as DOMA (Defense of Marriage Act) wouldn't even need to exist because the church would have taken all power to license marriage out of the hands of the state and bring it into the hands of the Body of Christ where it belongs in the first place!

These, and many more reasons listed below are why we here at The Empowerment Center, wish to see every Christian church in America reorganized properly with a Corporation Sole.

As you will read using the facts to follow, today, the Corporation Sole may very well represent itself as the modern day savior of churches from government rules and restrictions.

Chapter 3 – THE CHURCH ESTABLISHMENT AFFIDAVIT (and WHY it is so vital to your Church/Ministry)

When getting a Corporation Sole for your Church and Ministry, it is important to note that your actually creating two separate legal creatures. First, you create your Church *(which is legally manifested through a Church Establishment Affidavit)* and then the Churches subsequent Corporation Sole *(which is nothing more than an isolated and incorporated office title position held within the Church for the purposes of managing all of the Churches financial assets and is NOT the Church itself).* A Corporation Sole CANNOT be established unless your Church is first created through the use of a Church Establishment Affidavit. This unique affidavit needs to be signed by both you as the Pastor of the Church, Two Church member witnesses and your Churches eventual Corporation Sole's Successor and/or Secretary. If a Corporation Sole were to be established prior to you signing, witnessing and having notarized the Church Affidavit, then your Corporation Sole can be out of statutory compliance and potentially deemed a *sham organization* by the IRS and courts.

The reason we emphasis that a Church must first be organized through a Church Establishment Affidavit, is because an Affidavit is the highest form of evidence a person can bring forth into a Federal courtroom. It is considered the supreme truth until proven otherwise. This allows your ministry to prove to the court, *without a reasonable doubt,* the distinct legal existence of your Church, it's MANDATORY tax exemption jurisdiction under the law of 26 USC 508(c)(1)(a), it creates a record that is signed under the penalties of perjury by multiple Church members and declares that your Church even lawfully fulfills the IRS and courts own 14 point standard to even be legally recognized as a Church! It's creation and use also allows the Church to create a legal and jurisdictional separation of responsibilities between the role of the Church itself and the isolated and incorporated office of the Corporation Sole (which the latter is under 501c3's jurisdiction).

THE JURISDICTIONAL DISTINCTIONS BETWEEN THE LAW OF BOTH 26 USC 508(C)(1)(A) AND 501(C)(3) IN THEIR RELATIONSHIP TO A CHURCH ESTABLISHMENT AFFIDAVIT

In order to better understand everything, let's first discuss the IRS's Jurisdiction over both 508c1a and 501c3. You'll begin to see WHY creating your Church with a Church Establishment Affidavit and then organizing it's finances through a subsequent Corporation Sole, is the only viable way to creating a Church here in America.

First lets look at the law of 508c1a and what entities it has jurisdiction over:

26 USC 508(c)(1)(a) gives a MANDATORY Tax Exemption status to Churches without any pre-conditions *(Unlike 501c3's stipulations of barring religious organizations from all political activity)*.

Therefor, 508c1a has Jurisdiction over:

Churches, their integrated auxiliaries, and conventions or associations of churches and any organization which is not a private foundation and the gross receipts of which in each taxable year are normally not more than $5,000. A Church organized with the use of a Church Establishment Affidavit is underneath the jurisdiction of 508c1a. This type of Church is what I would like to call a FREE CHURCH. It's a Church that has now been set free from the bondage and political restrictions of 501c3.

While 501c3 only has Jurisdiction over:
Corporations, Certain Trusts, Community Chests, Funds and Foundations. You notice that the word CHURCH is completely absent from this list? That's because Churches are NOT subject 501c3 rules. Only religious organizations that have incorporated themselves are underneath 501c3's jurisdiction. Churches are only mentioned under the jurisdiction of the law of 508c1a. It is

generally misunderstood among many legal professionals that ALL Churches are generally always under the classification of 501c3. This is a misconception because nearly 99% of all Churches are fully incorporated (thus automatically fall under the Corporate designation of 501c3). Since a Church being formed through an affidavit and being declared under 508(c)(1)(a) as neither being considered a Corporation, community chest, religious trust, fund or foundation, then its designation under 501c3 DOES NOT APPLY.

Now, unlike 508c1a that gives the Church mandatory tax exemption, 501c3's tax exemption status is only guaranteed if the religious organization meets the conditions set forth in 501c3.

These Restrictions for Incorporated Religious Organizations Include:

#1. No part of the net earnings of which inures to the benefit of any private shareholder or individual:

This is WHY Churches are forced into having a board of directors *(aka Polity Body, Board of Elders, Board of Deacons and etc)*. A Corporation Sole is the only exception to this rule. It does not require an oversight committee to manage its assets.

All other religious organizations, religious trusts, community chests funds and foundations are subjected to this IRS rule and are legally required to have a voting committee/board. In this case, rights of the State of Oregon trump the Federal Governments desire to force the Church to have a voting board.

#2. No substantial part of the activities of which is carrying on propaganda and which does not participate in, or intervene in *(including the publishing or distributing of statements)*, **any political campaign on behalf of** *(or in opposition to)* **any candidate for public office:**

This absolutely satanic law means your incorporated Church or religious trust CANNOT engage in or influence any aspect of public policy for any reason whatsoever. Completely defeating the intent of the Church achieving its purpose of fulfilling Romans 8:20-21.

This is why the Church Establishment Affidavit is so important. Only Corporations (that means ANY incorporated Church or religious organization), Trusts (that means ANY form of a religious trust), community chests, funds and/or foundations are AUTOMATICALLY declared under the jurisdiction of 501c3. Since the Church Affidavit is neither one of the things listed above, it is completely immune to 501c3 and thus places your Church under the jurisdiction of the law of 508c1a. Without this jurisdictional distinction between the Church itself (created through the Church Establishment Affidavit) and the office of the Corporation Sole (which is incorporated as a 501c3 for banking purposes) then it would be impossible under current US law to organize a ministry using any other method (outside of the properly utilizing both an affidavit and a Corporation Sole).

WHY OUR CHURCH ESTABLISHMENT AFFIDAVIT IS SO IMPORTANT TO CHURCHES

We should note that the Church Establishment Affidavit we've created here at The Empowerment Center was crafted in such a manner that it accomplishes the following:

1.) It lawfully fulfills ALL 14 Points the IRS and courts require Churches to have in order to be legally recognized as a Church by the Federal Government. *Read more about the IRS's 14 points later in the book.*

2.) It distinctly declares the jurisdictional distinction and differences between the office, title and roles of the Church itself, the office of the Sr. Pastor (which both are under the law of 508c1a) and the Office of the Corporation Sole (which is solely under 501c3) *This is THE KEY to the ultimate victory over 501c3 and gender law restrictions!*
3.) It uniquely declares your Corporation Sole's intended future Successor and it defines who fulfills the role of it's intended Secretary.
4.) It allows for two additional Church members to declare and affirm the existence of the said Church/Ministry.
5.) It declares the Churches recognition of being under the law of both the mandatory tax exemption law of 26 USC 508(c)(1)(a) and the mandatory exemption from filing law 26 USC 6033(3)(a)(I-III).
6.) It declares that it does NOT find it advantageous to seek official recognition from the IRS for the Churches tax exemption status and rejects the IRS's form 1023.
7.) It removes all doubts and puts an end to any conflicting decision regarding your Churches distinct legal existence.
8.) The Bank will use it to validate the role of the Successor in the event of the Corporation Sole's demise and or resignation.
9.) It strictly prohibits same sex marriage, it declares that the LGBT lifestyle is against God's will, it restricts the employment, volunteer assignment or appointment of LGBT person(s) and it also helps protect your facilities from being obligated to host LGBT events.

DOES THE GOVERNMENT OR IRS REALLY WANT THIS FIGHT?

To the best of our knowledge, prior to us writing the Book and setting the record straight on the Corporation Sole, no one had ever thought to use an unincorporated Church Establishment Affidavit to both manifest the Church but also outline the jurisdictional distinction between the Church itself and the isolated office of the Corporation Sole. Then use the Church that is under the law of 26 USC 508(c)(1)(a) and NOT the 501c3 Corporation Sole to conduct operations that could influence public policy or resist the gay agenda.

There is an argument to be made that a Church can perform and operate in this manner and not become subjected to 501c3 political restrictions (since the affidavit clearly outlines the different jurisdictions). In fact, it would be the only argument the Church could legally make since every other method a Church uses to incorporate or manage it's finances places it underneath 501c3's jurisdiction. We understand that this puts us in a position where there is no prior legal precedence for this type of legal claim. That is good for several reasons: If the IRS really wanted that fight and wanted to disprove that the said Church in this claim (Let's use our Church, The Empowerment Center, as an example) is in fact NOT a Church, they are going to need to be able to disprove our affidavit (which is vital to our argument that our Church is indeed a Church) is false. They would have several problems in this area. First, they would need to prove that everyone on the affidavit was lying (and thus committed the penalties of perjury). This would be especially difficult since it is VERY difficult for any Judge or IRS official to have the proper regulatory authority to even legally define a Church (one might even say to legally define a Church is unconstitutional in and of itself)! Now, the IRS has in place what they consider a 14 point test to see whether or not a Church is a legitimate Church. The principles of this test are used by the IRS and courts to determine if a Church is just that, a Church. Never mind that in the very same report the authors make the very wise statement that we will HEAVILY be using in any defense,

"Given the variety of religious practice, the determination of what constitutes a church is inherently unquantifiable. Attempts to use a dogmatic numerical approach might unconstitutionally favor established churches at the expense of newer, less traditional institutions." – IRS 14 point rule guide.

Here at The Empowerment Center and ChurchFreedom.org, we recognized this opening and took all 14 points to the IRS and courts own preferences and applied them within the framework of our affidavit. It's important that we did this, as this should be enough to satisfy their very own discrepancies since a minimum of 4-5 people are coming together and attesting to these facts under the penalties of perjury, facts that any lawful Church could easily prove. This leaves only the isolated Corporation Sole as the lone bearer of the 501c3 status and not the Church itself. <u>This means the Corporation Sole</u> (which is the only entity underneath 501c3's jurisdiction) <u>needs to be the sole party responsible for any alleged violations to the 501c3 principle</u> (which again, should only be limited to the 501c3 Corporate Sole and NOT the 508c1a Church). In addition, we would also take a play from the Alliance Defending Freedom's, Pulpit Freedom Sunday's playbook as well and argue a secondary point that in their words,

"For instance, if a church loses its tax-exempt status for the pastor speaking from the pulpit, there is an argument to be made that because the church is automatically exempt under section 508(c)(1) (A) of the Internal Revenue Code, the tax-exempt status is only lost for the day the sermon was preached, and any contributions made at other times would still be deductible. It is important to note that this argument has not been tested and taxpayers should seek professional advice before claiming any such deduction for itemization." – From, Pulpit Freedom Sunday and The Alliance Defending Freedom

Making such bold argument(s) for legitimate Churches could potentially set a VERY REAL and VERY SERIOUS precedence if the Federal Government failed to make their case to a Judge or Jury. If they challenge our argument that Churches operating under the law of 26 USC 508(c)(1)(a), *not the Churches subsequent and isolated Corporation Sole*, can influence politics, have the Church body vote for or against political candidates, have the Church lobby congress or have the Church distribute political propaganda on behalf or against any political candidate for office (once again, the Church and NOT the 501c3 isolated Corporation Sole) and they lose, then they will potentially open the door WIDE OPEN for EVERY SINGLE CHURCH IN AMERICA to RUN to get their Corporation Sole and be SET FREE from the political restrictions that have plagued our nations Churches. If they win such an argument, by the time they win we would have already freely given away our Corporation Sole support to TEN'S OF THOUSANDS of CHURCHES that already HATE 501c3 with a passion and are already bold enough to speak unfiltered truth behind the pulpit. This could mean EXTREME backlash from potentially millions of registered voters from members of those congregations (many of whom are EXTREMELY influential Christian business men and politicians themselves) that we've been training Pastors in how to lead in influencing intended Christian reforms. Also, to unwisely make enemies with the Church in a political season such as this with the IRS already embroiled in scandal after scandal (from Lois Lerner lying to Congress to the IRS 'accidentally' destroying all hard drive evidence) or a Justice Department that fails to enforce current laws or investigate any Government agency of any wrongdoing, it would leave a VERY bad taste in the mouth of Christian voters in these Churches and would propel us to the National Spotlight (which is EXACTLY what we want, so we can make our case to Christians everywhere). It would also be extremely unwise timing as they would have underestimated the Jury's potential disdain for the Government and their routine MANY failures, cover-ups and current violations to oaths of office perceived by the American public by officials in the Federal Government (this is in addition to the fact, that we will call upon the several hundred eye witnesses and VERY Charismatic Pastors that will first hand testify that we're a Church). Any one person being on that Jury that is either a Republican or Christian WILL side with us. This would give the Church a HUGE edge in court. Either way, wisdom would see that such a challenge (if ever) given by the Government based on these merits would end up being a lose/lose situation for them.

Now, this does not mean the Government is our enemy nor should we treat them as an enemy (because they're not our enemy). They are just public servants upholding their oaths to defend a law that should have never been implemented in the first place. Just like how slavery or segregation used to be valid "laws", that didn't make them right or righteous and they needed to be repealed, 501c3 also needs to be fully repealed. This is going to need to take Churches working with Congress, the Senate and The Office of The President in order to repeal this satanic law. Congress is really where the Church needs to focus their attention on and mobilize together as it is not our intent to pick a fight with the Government nor give the Federal Government the impression that the Church has an anti-government stance (because we don't). On the contrary, the Church is here to love and mutually edify both the Government and Society in general. We represent the Nations moral center that we help guide it's people through the ages by reminding them to love The Lord with all of their body, soul and spirit and to love each other as we love ourselves. Without us teaching his love and direction, the world begins to descend into the darkness and chaos as we see it in today.

This is WHY we do whatever it takes to freely give our support to as many qualified approved Churches in the shortest time as humanly possible. Officials should know and understand that while other unscrupulous Corporation Sole peddlers have fallen to greed and tried to sell the Corporation Sole away as a mere tax shelter, we have not. We ABSOLUTELY NEVER give our support to individuals or entities looking to create a tax shelter. If a person cannot get at least 4 living people over the age of 21 that are willing to sign an affidavit under the penalties of perjury that they are a bona fide Church that lives up to the IRS and courts own 14 point test, then we deny their application at ChurchFreedom.org immediately. We've denied more applications than anyone knows with individuals trying to offer us everything you can think of for access to our support and we've denied ALL OF THEIR ATTEMPTS. If we even remotely smell someone coming that gives us the impression that they are either an individual trying to evade lawful taxes owed or an undercover informant trying to entrap us with promises of money, power or prestige for giving them our ministry and Corporation Sole support, we not only deny their application but we also permanently prohibit their access to our website by blocking their unique IP address. We ONLY work with legitimate BONA FIDE Churches.

This is why we need your help to spread the word about ChurchFreedom.org! We want to freely help support EVERY SINGLE Christian Church here in America. With your help, we've been able to directly support thousands of new Christian Churches this year alone. With your help, we can help FREE America's Churches from 501c3 entirely.

CHAPTER 4 – EASY INSTRUCTIONS FOR HOW TO QUICKLY SET UP BOTH YOUR CHURCH AND IT'S SUBSEQUENT CORPORATION SOLE

EXTREMELY IMPORTANT: DO NOT DEVIATE FROM THESE INSTRUCTIONS IN ANYWAY SHAPE OR FORM, IF YOU DO IT WILL NOT BE GOOD AND YOU CAN FACE UNNECESSARY TAXATION, FINES, PENALTIES, FORFEITURE OF ASSETS AND POTENTIAL IMPRISONMENT. Do everything we minister you to do in this process down to the letter.

Step #1 Modify, Sign, Witness and have Notarized Your Official Church Establishment Affidavit:

In order to download an editable MS Word version of our Church Establishment Affidavit, please go to the following webpage:

www.ChurchFreedom.org/apply

Once your application is approved, you will be instructed to download and open this document. Please use the "find and replace" feature and find and replace the following fields:

- **Pastors Name Here:** Replace this with whomever will be the Overseer of the both the Church and the Corporation Sole.
- **Pastors Spouse:** Replace this with whomever your Successor and Secretary is going to be.
- **SUCCESSOR NAME HERE:** ONLY Replace this with someone that you've elected to use as the Successor to the Corporation Sole.
- **SECRETARY NAME HERE:** ONLY Replace this with someone that you've elected to use as the Secretary to the Corporation Sole.
- **Church Name Here:** Replace with the name of your Church. If you already have a prior Church established,

then please read our book for full details in how to properly reorganize your ministry.
- **Witness #1:** Replace with the name of your first witness. **IMPORTANT:** An individual that has either created their own Corporation Sole or signed any other Church affidavit as a Church Member CANNOT SIGN YOUR CHURCH AFFIDAVIT. Instead of listing them as a Church Member, you will need to change the wording to: Declarant.
- **Witness #2:** Replace with the name of your second witness.
- **IMPORTANT:** An individual that has either created their own Corporation Sole or signed any other Church affidavit as a Church Member CANNOT SIGN YOUR CHURCH AFFIDAVIT. Instead of listing them as a Church Member, you will need to change the wording to: Declarant.

IMPORTANT: The ONLY other change I will allow on this affidavit is if you would like to change the name of Jesus on the Affidavit to Yeshua Ha-Mashiach (Christ's true name for proper interpretation). Other than that, no other modifications are allowed unless given express written permission by Joshua Kenny-Greenwood (the Overseer of The Empowerment Center).

Once you have signed, witnessed and notarized your Church Affidavit, then count yourselves blessed and highly favored! You are now one of the very few Churches not under the law of 501c3 where now you can finally enjoy being able to preach without any boundaries whatsoever and can influence public policy. The Federal Government can NOT do anything regarding the messages your Church preaches on Sunday morning anymore. You are also now ready to go to STEP #2!

Step #2 Get a Registered Agent:

Of the 7 remaining states that have active Corporation Sole laws, we recommend you applying to use us as your registered agent or going through Alaska (as they have the very best Corporation Sole laws, with California having the worst Corporation Sole law). If you need a Oregon registered agent, please consider freely applying for ministry support at:
www.ChurchFreedom.org/Apply
Unfortunately, because many people have used the Corporation Sole for its unintended purpose as a tax shelter (to hide lawful taxed owed to the Federal Government) nearly every single registered agent company in a state that has a Corporation Sole law will not take on Corporation Sole clients. They consider them too high risk for fraud and abuse. Therefor, we highly recommend applying with us so that we can help assist your Church and or ministry. Please apply at:
www.ChurchFreedom.org/apply

Step #3 Get your Corporation Sole's EIN number, Bank Accounts and Subsequent Tax Exempted PayPal Account (for receiving donations online):

Once you get the Certified Copy of your Articles of Incorporation back from the state you apply in, then you will need to go online and get an IRS EIN number for your Corporation Sole (which takes all of 3 minutes). To do this, simply go to: www.irs.gov/Businesses/Small-Businesses-%26-Self-Employed/Apply-for-an-Employer-Identification-Number-(EIN)-Online ***Note: Their new hours of operation are Monday through Friday 7:00 a.m. to 10:00 p.m. Eastern time.*
Just in case the link above does not work, do a Google Search for the following, "How to apply for an EIN online"

You will want to select, "**View Additional Types, Including Tax-Exempt and Governmental Organizations**". This will be a "**Church Controlled Organization**" for "Banking Purposes" only. Then you will need to select **"INDIVIDUAL"** and input your name, SSI and address for mailing notices. Make sure that you DO NOT use the name of your Church but rather the Corporation

Sole. Remember, your not getting an EIN for the Church (we want to fully un-incorporate that so it doesn't come under the 501c3 law). If you have a prior Church set up with an EIN and your reorganizing everything with the new Church and Corporation Sole, your old EIN will become obsolete. Once completed, you will be issued the EIN number.

HOW TO SET UP A BANK ACCOUNT FOR THE CORPORATION SOLE:

We HIGHLY recommend that you go to either Bank of America or Wells Fargo because they have both confirmed for us that all you need is both the EIN and the Articles of Incorporation and no other documentation in order to set up your bank account. If you live in State of Mississippi, or if you encounter any issue with the bank whatsoever, the most common resolution to any issue is to file your Corporation Sole as a foreign corporation with your resident state. By doing so, it typically resolves any banking issue. To find out more on how to file your Corporation Sole as a foreign corporation, please contact your local Secretary of States office for more details, as we do not currently offer ongoing support for filing as a foreign Corporation for your state.

SET UP YOUR CORPORATION SOLE'S TAX EXEMPTED PAYPAL ACCOUNT:

For PayPal, they require the following items listed below to consider you a "Tax Exempt" entity. Remember, you're not a "non-profit" nor "for-profit" entity. A church and its Corporation Sole are a TAX EXEMPTED entity.

PayPal requires the following (this is the letter they send to you when you sign up as a tax exempt entity with them):

Dear Corporation Sole, We are writing to you in regards to your PayPal Account. PayPal appreciates that you have chosen us to accept payments for your organization. As part of PayPal's Compliance Program, we request that entities wishing to accept donations on behalf of a charity or other non-profit organization provide evidence of their legitimacy.

Please provide the following information:

- Your registration as a non-profit organization with any applicable regulatory body governing your jurisdiction, such as your organization's certified Articles of Incorporation filed with your Secretary of State or your IRS 501(c)(3) determination letter. ***(For this, simply send them a certified copy of your articles of incorporation.)***
- The link to confirm your organization's registration status online (if applicable). ***(Send them a possible link to your Corporation Sole's registration status online with that state's Secretary of State Office website.)***
- Information about the nature of your organization and the type of payments you intend to process with PayPal. ***(Tell them that you're a church and will be intending to receive tax-deductible offerings.)***
- A copy of a bank statement or a voided check with theorganization's name and organization address pre-printed on it from each bank account that you intend to attach to this PayPal Account. Each bank account that you attach to this PayPal Account must be under the ownership of the Charity/Non-Profit Organization (NPO) and cannot be a personal bank account. ***(This is easy, simply give them a check from the newly formed bank account that is in the name of the Corporation Sole.)***
- A brief organizational summary or Mission Statement. ***(Send them your vision statement. Here is an example of my own vision statement:***

The Empowerment Center Vision Statement:

Vision Statement:
The vision of The Empowerment Center is reaching out in redeeming love and liberating power, bringing the Word of God to all people, of all ages, and all socio-economic backgrounds.

(Handwritten note: Use this statement)

- Wealth
- Womanhood
- Wisdom
- The Word
- Family

Mission Statement:
Our Mission is to initiate and promote a "Kingdom Shift" mindset.

A 'Kingdom Shift Mindset' is a Holy Spirit empowered **mindset** shift from fear to hope, from rejection to acceptance, from chaos to peace, from ignorance to empowerment, from lack to favor and from condemnation to grace. This mission is also here to help break religious interdenominational barriers and to equip His people for works of service, so that the body of Christ may be built up, until we all reach unity in the faith and in the knowledge of the Son of God and become mature, attaining to the whole measure of the fullness of Christ.".

- *Subordination letter from the parent organization (if applicable). **(This is non-applicable (unless you're underneath the authority of another FREE CHURCH.)**

All requested information must be submitted within 30 days to continue the review process.

That's all PayPal requires. They should easily set this up for you to be fully active in 3-5 days. Then you may begin to receive tithes and offerings from all over the world via the Internet!

Chapter 5 – Legal Facts, Questions and Answers Related to the Corporation Sole

The following is a list of typical questions we have received from thousands of Pastors from across America. We've attempted to compile them all into this chapter to help you easily understand all aspects of the Corporation Sole. If you have an original question that is not listed here, please submit it via our website by going to: **www.ChurchFreedom.org/support**. Once we have received your question, we will answer our sites frequently asked questions page here: **www.ChurchFreedom.org/faqs**

QUESTIONS AND ANSWERS:

What are the 7 States that still have active Corporation Sole laws?
Answer: They are: California, Arizona, Alaska, Hawaii, Montana, Colorado and Wyoming. DO NOT BE DISCOURAGED if you do not live in one of these 7 States because you can easily apply with us online to represent you and if you complete our instructions for the state in which we reside, your certified articles of incorporation will be completely accepted by your native state through common law. Very soon with your help, we can begin lobbying each state to form its own unique Corporation Sole law!

What if there are church members in a different state, can they still sign our Affidavit?
Answer: Yes. Even though I answered this above, I want to reiterate that if you have a church member that lives in a different state who wishes to sign your affidavit, then you will need to mail them the affidavit, have them sign it in front of a public notary and then have them send it back to you directly.

What are common mistakes churches make when establishing themselves, mistakes that erroneously place them under the jurisdiction of 501c3?

Answer: Almost too many to count! Firstly, nearly 98% of churches organized today in the United States of America have voluntarily rescinded their status as even being defined as a church and have instead opted to be considered both *"creatures of the state"* and or a *"religious organization"*. There are several ways a church makes these disastrous mistakes:

Mistake #- 1 A church "Incorporates" their ministry: This is a common mistake due chiefly to a bank requiring that in order to open up an account, they would like to see the church registered as an incorporation with their Secretary of State's office. What the senior minister may fail to realize is, the instant a church incorporates its self, it now is lawfully defined as a "creature of the state" and is then no longer even legally recognized as a church.

This is pursuant to United States Supreme Court ruling "Hale v Henkle" which Chief Justice Melville Fuller states: *"A corporation is a creature of the state. It is presumed to be incorporated for the benefit of the public. It receives certain special privileges and franchises and holds them subject to the laws of the state and the limitation of its charter. Its powers are limited by law. It can make no contract not authorized by its charter. Its rights to act as a corporation are only preserved to it so long as it obeys the laws of its creation. There is a reserved right in the legislature to investigate its contracts and ascertain if it has exceeded its powers."*

Also, since incorporations fall directly under the jurisdiction of 501c3, the church is now considered by law to be defined as a "religious organization". A *Bona Fide* church under the Jurisdiction of 26 U.S.C § 508(c)(1)(a) is NOT incorporated at all nor is it allowed to be incorporated. Once a church makes this first common fatal mistake, they have (whether through ignorance of the law or their own acquiescence) completely rescinded their rights to be considered a *bona fide* church, and are now entirely under the terrible jurisdiction of 501c3.

On a side note: Since a Corporation Sole is legally defined as a "natural person" according to the IRS, a Corporation Sole falls under the legal definition of an "individual" which is also described in US Common Law ruling Hale v Henkle which Chief Justice Melville Fuller states,

"The individual may stand upon his constitutional Rights as a citizen. He is entitled to carry on his private business in his own way. His power to contract is unlimited. He owes no such duty [to submit his books and papers for an examination] to the State, since he receives nothing therefrom, beyond the protection of his life and property. His Rights are such as existed by the law of the land [Common Law] long antecedent to the organization of the State, and can only be taken from him by due process of law, and in accordance with the Constitution. Among his Rights are a refusal to incriminate himself, and the immunity of himself and his property from arrest or seizure except under a warrant of the law. He owes nothing to the public so long as he does not trespass upon their Rights."

A "natural person" and an "individual" are defined by Blacks Law Dictionary 9th Edition as:

Person. (Be) 1. A human being. Also termed *natural person*.

Individual, *adj.* (I5c) 1. Existing as an indivisible entity. 2. For relating to a single person or thing, as opposed to a group.

There is a possible legal argument to be made that even though a Corporation Sole is registered with a Secretary of State as a corporation, that it in fact has the same rights as individual rights, which supersede corporate law. It is the only known corporation in American law to do this.

Mistake #2- A church seeks, "Official Recognition of Tax Exemption" from the IRS (i.e. they fill out an IRS form 1023) and/or they assume that if they do not, "apply" for 501c3 status, that they are somehow immune from the 501c3 law and it's jurisdiction: 98% of organized churches in the United States of America have sought official recognition of tax exemption from the IRS. Churches have erroneously filed an IRS form 1023 to accomplish this. It's EXTREMELY IMPORTANT to note that seeking official recognition of tax exemption from the IRS and filing a form 1023 is the absolute WORST POSSIBLE mistake a church can make when organizing itself.

Firstly, pursuant to 26 U.S.C § 508(c)(1)(a), a church was NEVER required to notify the Treasury Department of their tax exempt status to begin with! They were automatically exempt simply for the fact that they were a church!

Here is what 26 U.S.C § 508(c)(1)(a) actually says,

New organizations must notify Secretary that they are applying for recognition of section 501(c)(3) status Except as provided in subsection (c), an organization organized after October 9, 1969, shall not be treated as an organization described in section 501 (c)(3)—
(c) Exceptions
(1) Mandatory exceptions
Subsections (a) and (b) shall not apply to—
(A) churches, their integrated auxiliaries, and conventions or associations of churches, or
(B) any organization which is not a private foundation (as defined in section 509 (a)) and the gross receipts of which in each taxable year are normally not more than $5,000.

So, understand that when it states, "new organizations MUST notify the Treasury" that the official notification IS the IRS form 1023. ALL organizations besides churches and private foundations with net earning less then $5,000 are required by law to file this form 1023 to seek approval of their tax-exempt status. Churches were NEVER required or lawfully compelled to file this form.

You might ask, "Why is filing a form 1023 so terrible?" Well for starters, prior to signing the form 1023 and pursuant to 26 U.S.C § 6033(3)(A)(1-3), your church was previously <u>mandatorily</u> exempted from even being required to file annual informational returns to the IRS! Now if a church has signed the form 1023, they have contractually obligated themselves to file their annual informational reports with the IRS consecutively every three years and if they refuse, they will have their tax-exempt status automatically revoked! Understand: Your church was previously MANDATORILY exempted from filing and now instead you've contractually agreed to not only file, but if you fail to file consecutively every three years you will automatically lose your entire tax exempt status and will be required to reapply with the IRS.

In addition, not only has your church ceased being considered a church at this point (and now only considered a religious organization) it has contractually obligated itself to the Treasury Department with ALL the provisions of 501c3. This was the very reason why Branch Ministries with Dan Little as their pastor were the first church in America to ever loose its tax-exempt status for engaging in the distribution of political propaganda (*in the Federal Court of Appeals Case BRANCH MINISTRIES and Dan Little, Pastor, Appellants, v. Charles O. ROSSOTTI, Commissioner, Internal Revenue Service, Appellee*).

The presiding judge stated in his final judgment,

*"Branch Ministries, Inc. operates the church at Pierce Creek ("church"), a Christian church located in Binghamton, New York. In 1983, **the church requested** and received a letter from the IRS recognizing its tax-exempt status."*

You see, the church (Branch Ministries) even though it was already tax exempt, erroneously sought recognition of their tax exempt status and thus entered into a <u>contractual agreement</u> with the IRS.

*"The church appears to assume that the withdrawal of a **<u>conditional privilege</u>** for failure to meet the condition is in itself an unconstitutional burden on its free exercise right."*

Do you see? The instant Branch Ministries applied for official recognition via the IRS form 1023, it accepted that where previously their tax-exempt status was mandatorily exempted, that now it was a dependent upon several *"conditional privileges"*. Regardless, if the decision on behalf of Branch ministries to voluntarily waive their legal rights by signing the form 1023 was due to their lack of knowledge or understanding of the law itself, it didn't matter. When Branch ministries tried to argue that loosing their tax-exempt status was unconstitutional, the presiding judge ruled, *"We find this argument more creative than persuasive."* This was due to the fact that very simply, when Branch Ministries filed the form 1023, they signed a legal CONTRACT that stipulated they wouldn't engage in political activities and then when they violated the terms of the contract then their tax exemption status was revoked, and they had no legal recourse!

Also, the only two conditional privileges that a church receives from the federal government when they sign a form 1023 are that they get reduced rates on postage stamps and that they have the ability to <u>apply</u> for federal grants. That's it. The church then waives all its rights to even being considered a church, they waive their rights to be exempted from taxes without conditions, they waive their rights from being mandatorily exempted from filing annual information returns, they waive their rights to engage in politics, they waive their rights to distribute political propaganda, they waive their rights to influence legislation, they waive their rights to advocate who their congregations should or should not vote for on election day, all for nothing more then being able to get better rates on postage stamps and the ability to <u>apply</u> for federal grants. The worst part of all: 98% of churches in America have done this! It brings a whole new meaning to when Paul wrote in 1st Timothy 1:7, *"They want to be teachers of the law, but they do not know what they are talking about or what they so confidently affirm!"* or better yet, *"my people perish for their lack of knowledge"* Hosea 4:6

Even if a church avoids these two major mistakes, the overwhelming problem is that, without a church organizing itself with a Corporation Sole, it is currently impossible to organize itself financially and NOT be under the jurisdiction of 501c3. In this case, the Corporation Sole is the saving grace for the church in this hour of need.

Even if a church decided to get very legally savvy and attempt to create their own version of our affidavit and then even get an unincorporated certified trust from a CPA or Attorney (which does not require an Federal Tax EIN number) in order to establish its bank accounts, it would STILL be considered a 'community chest, fund or foundation' according to the IRS and therefor come under the jurisdiction of the 501c3 law.

Also, there is a common misconception among pastors that if they do not apply for a 501c3 that somehow that makes them immune to the law and of the jurisdiction of 501c3. This could not be further from the truth. As I explained prior, the instant a church either incorporates itself, gets a Federal Tax Identification Number (including but not limited to an EIN number), creates a financial trust, asset holdings entity, bank account (checking or savings) or even gets an unincorporated certified trust from either an attorney or CPA, then the entirety of the church AUTOMATICALLY falls 100% under the jurisdiction of the law of 26 U.S.C § 501(c)(3).

This is why the Corporation Sole is so powerful, because it lawfully separates the jurisdiction of the church from its incorporated office bank accounts (thereby bringing the church under the jurisdiction of 26 U.S.C § 508(c)(1)(a) instead of the

501c3 law.) No other method outside of a Corporation Sole can accomplish this feat.

Can a church reorganize its current 501c3 status in favor of a Corporation Sole?

Answer: Absolutely! However, be warned: Before they do, the leaders involved will need to learn three important things: Discuss, Donate and Dissolve. Let me explain:

1. **Discuss:** Due to a 26 U.S.C § 501(c)(3) provision that, "no part of the net earnings of which inures to the benefit of any private shareholder or individual" clause, EVERY 501c3 church in America is required to have a polity body (i.e. board of elders, board of directors, board of trustees, church congregational vote, appropriations committee and etc.). They will need to seek approval of the dissolution of the current 501c3 status in favor of the reorganized church that will be under the jurisdiction of the 508c1a law instead. Many times, this will mean that the elders (or whoever the polity body is) will be required to vote them-selves out of office (this is not always an easy thing to do). These discussions will need to be very Holy Spirit led and handled with great care and wisdom on the behalf of the senior pastor wanting to reorganize the ministry. More times than I can count, the spirit of manipulation rears its ugly head (typically in the form of either a religious leader or wealthy donor that's been elected to a position in the church with voting rights). I have witnessed (more times than I care to count) situations where a pastor is fired within 24 hours of telling their church polity body about the Corporation Sole. This is because most polity bodies would seek to manipulate the churches finances into whatever direction THEY think is most appropriate instead of relying on the Holy Spirit's revelation, vision and discretion utilized by

the senior pastor of the church, which is the way God originally intended it.

This is another anti-kingdom side effect of the 501c3 law. It brought democracy into the body of Christ where it was never intended to function. God does NOT rule heaven through popular vote and neither should churches be run that same way. It is the role of the senior pastor to be the visionary of the house and to equip the saints. I would advise the pastor or senior person of the church getting the Corporation Sole to explain in detail to the elders or body polity that he/she will always consider their counsel prior to making a huge decision (especially since once the Corporation Sole is in place, there will be no church treasurer nor polity body with active voting rights anymore). This way, it will calm any concerns that the polity body may have prior to approval of the church's 501c3 dissolution.

2. **Donate:** ALL assets should be donated to the custody of the new Corporate Sole prior to final dissolution. This means any and all titles (such as property or vehicles), ownership custody of materials such as church pews, projectors and even financial assets (bank accounts, stocks, bonds, etc.) should be donated to the custody of the Corporate Sole prior to final dissolution. For each item of significant value, I would recommend that you draft (on church letterhead) an itemized donation letter from the prior church to the new Corporate Sole. Then, write a receipt of acknowledgement from the new Corporate Sole to the older church upon receipt of the donated items/assets. This way, there is a clear paper trail from one entity to another. This needs to be done <u>completely</u> prior to the final administrative dissolution of your old church's 501c3.

3. **Dissolve:** Once ALL prior church assets have been donated to the new Corporate Sole, then the original church should go through a thorough dissolution of its

corporate entity. It should contact any mother church (the parent 501c3) that's over its covering and resign from their covering or contact the Secretary of State to administratively dissolve the legal corporate entity of the prior church (including any DBA's as well). It will need to close all subsequent bank accounts for the prior church in favor of the Corporate Sole's new bank account. The church being formed under the "Church Establishment Affidavit" will be the supreme entity and the Corporate Sole will be the final legal asset holdings entity for all activities within the newly re-organized church.

This process can take several weeks depending on how complex the polity body has organized itself. I cannot reiterate enough, how much a senior pastor needs to prayerfully consider how and when to approach the polity body in regards to the Corporation Sole. I have heard of many pastors being fired within hours of introducing the Corporate Sole structure, because they did not fully have their houses in order. Even if it takes a few weeks, it is better to get the whole church in order, than to begin premature discussions regarding the Corporation Sole.

If I get a Corporation Sole, will my church be considered a 501c3?

Answer: Not at all! Remember that there are two Tax Exempt Laws in our Country. The first is 26 U.S.C § 508(c)(1)(a) and the other is 26 U.S.C § 501(c)(3). Your church will be a completely separate legal entity from your Corporate Sole and will be under the jurisdiction of 26 U.S.C § 508(c)(1)(a) NOT 501c3. Here at The Empowerment Center and our website ChurchFreedom.org, we help lawfully establish your church first (prior to helping you organize your Corporation Sole) by giving you access to our custom Church Establishment Affidavit. This is a legal affidavit that is signed by you and nearly 4+ witnesses (all under the penalty of perjury) that lawfully establishes you as a *bona fide* church pursuant to the Federal Law of 26 U.S.C § 508(c)(1)(a) which grants your church mandatory tax exemption without any pre-conditions and is completely separate from the jurisdiction of 501c3.

If our church decides to reorganize with a Corporate Sole, can our church itself (not it's Corporation Sole) be actively involved in political propaganda, attempt to influence legislation or publish political statements on behalf of (or in opposition to) any candidate for public office?
Answer: Absolutely YES! Because of the enormity of this issue, please let me explain this in great detail. Remember, that there are two tax exempt laws related to churches and or religious organizations in this country. The first is 26 U.S.C § 508(c)(1)(a) and other is 26 U.S.C § 501(c)(3). Per the 1st Amendment of the Constitution, you have the constitutional right to express your religious beliefs. However, because tax exemption is not written into our Federal Constitution, then all exemptions are considered "privileges" rather then a constitutional Right. Now, each of the laws listed above are considered privileges, however, only one of those laws has conditions to the privilege of tax exemption. A church organized under 26 U.S.C § 508(c)(1)(a) contains absolutely NO conditions to their exempt status (they are mandatorily exempted by default simply for BEING a church). This means, that any church lawfully established under 26 U.S.C § 508(c)(1)(a) can engage in ANY political matter they wish without any fear whatsoever of loosing their tax exempt status. This is what makes a church that organizes with a Corporate Sole so powerful! It is the only known legal way in the United States code of laws where a church can truly organize itself under 26 U.S.C § 508(c)(1)(a) instead of having the entirety of the ministry organized under 501c3. This is due to the fact that before a Corporate Sole can be formed, there must first be a *bona fide* church already lawfully established. We help you do this with our Church Establishment Affidavit. This creates two distinct legal jurisdictions for your ministry. Even though a Corporation Sole is technically considered a 501c3, it acts

neither as you're church NOR you're ministry. It is nothing more than an incorporated office within a pre-established church for the purposes of being a asset holding entity. Once again, the Corporation Sole is neither your church nor ministry. When we preach on Sunday morning, or have political things to say, we do not say them under the authority of our bank account (which is the Corporate Sole)! We say them under the authority the Holy Spirit and our Church Establishment Affidavit. This creates a clear jurisdictional boundary that no other newly formed church could hope to have because every other church in America that does not organize with a Corporation Sole is considered a 501c3 the instant they either incorporate or establish a financial holdings entity in the name of the church itself. Remember, 501c3 is for religious organizations that form either through an incorporation, trust, community chest, fund or foundation. Even so called "508 trusts" or a church that creates an unincorporated certified trust from either a CPA or state licensed attorney will fall under this 501c3 category because the IRS will consider that trust to be either a "community chest, fund or foundation". The instant a church does this, the ENTIRETY of the church falls under the jurisdiction of 501c3 and they completely rescind their rights under 26 U.S.C § 508(c)(1)(a).

I will use our church as an example. The name of our church is "The Empowerment Center". This church is under the jurisdiction of 26 U.S.C § 508(c)(1)(a) because it was formed through a lawful affidavit (which is NOT considered either a incorporation, trust, community chest, fund or foundation,) therefor, it is excluded in its entirety from being considered under the jurisdiction of 501c3. The name of our subsequent Corporate Sole however, is, "The Empowerment Center Overseer and Successors, a Corporation Sole". You see how vastly different the names of those two entities are? Also, when getting an EIN number, you will NOT be getting an EIN for your church but rather for the Corporate Sole instead. These seemingly minor details create a titanic difference in your church's ability to fully be active in the political spectrum. Executed properly, your church will be able to actively be involved with political matters, influence legislation, lobby congress and put out material on behalf or against ANY political candidate running for public office. I cannot understate how powerful this difference is. If ALL churches in America reorganized properly with a Corporate Sole, there would be a gigantic shift in the church's authority in nearly ALL matters of government. From social issues such as gay marriage, abortion, and more, we would dominate the entire political spectrum and be able to speak truth. Currently The Body of Christ holds the largest block of registered voters in the country. This fact alone makes me want to help reorganize each church in America. This is why I need your help in placing this book into the hands of each pastor here in America. With your help, we can accomplish things that have not been seen since the 1968 Civil Rights Act (when the church effectively ended segregation here in America). We could see things change overnight for the better here in America.

What is the difference or advantages of the Corporation Sole versus a traditional 501c3?
Answer: The differences are fairly significant. First of all, unlike traditional 501c3 churches (those that cannot be active in politics whatsoever for fear of loosing their tax exempt status), a church that is organized financially with a Corporation Sole CAN operate politically without fear of loosing its exempt status. This is explained in great detail in our previous question, *"If our church decides to reorganize with a Corporate Sole, can our church be actively involved in political propaganda, attempt to influence legislation or publish political statements on behalf of (or in opposition to) any candidate for public office?"*

Secondly, a Corporate Sole, *unlike all other forms of 501c3 religious organizations,* requires NO board of directors, trustees or governing polity body. It requires no church treasurer and no by-laws. It is one of the only legal entities in United States law that acts as a natural person (while simultaneously acting as a tax exempt organization, asset holdings entity, business and more). Unlike a traditional 501c3 that has a church treasurer, the Corporation Sole acts as the "sole" office that handles ALL of the assets. This alone can liberate a senior minister that would typically be required to go through a church polity body's appropriations committee to get a popular vote on any new thing the senior minister would like to purchase or spend on the ministry in general.

Thirdly, pursuant to 26 U.S.C § 6033(3)(A)(1-3), churches and their subsequent Corporation Sole's are MANDATORILY exempted in federal law from filing annual informational returns! Currently, there is no federal law that 'lawfully compels' a Corporation Sole from having a ministerial stipend salary. In addition, because establishing a church does not require you filling out an IRS form 1023 seeking "official recognition" of your tax exempt status (*because no recognition was ever required pursuant to 26 U.S.C § 508c1a*) your church is NOT required to issue a minister's stipend salary (W2) nor file returns consecutively for three years or risk rescinding your tax exempt status completely (*unlike churches that HAVE sought official recognition of their tax exempt status from the IRS*).

Also, Since a Corporation Sole is legally defined as a "natural person" according to the IRS, a Corporation Sole falls under the legal definition of an "individual" which is also described in US Common Law ruling Hale v Henkle which Chief Justice Melville Fuller states:

"The individual may stand upon his constitutional Rights as a citizen. He is entitled to carry on his private business in his own way. His power to contract is unlimited. He owes no such duty [to submit his books and papers for an examination] to the State, since he receives nothing therefrom, beyond the protection of his life and property. His Rights are such as existed by the law of the land [Common Law] long antecedent to the organization of the State, and can only be taken from him by due process of law, and in accordance with the Constitution. Among his Rights are a refusal to incriminate himself, and the immunity of himself and his property from arrest or seizure except under a warrant of the law.

He owes nothing to the public so long as he does not trespass upon their Rights."

A natural person and an individual are defined by Blacks Law Dictionary 9th Edition as,

Person. (Be) 1. A human being. Also termed *natural person*.

Individual, *adj.* (I5c) 1. Existing as an indivisible entity. 2. For relating to a single person or thing, as opposed to a group.

These reasons alone are enough to send every pastor in America RUNNING to get their churches and subsequent Corporation Sole's established!

Can our church have a Corporate Sole even if we do not live in one of the 7 States that has Corporate Sole Laws?
Answer: YES. When you have us, or another registered agent, acting as your domiciled registered agent. Just like any corporation, many businesses decide that organizing in another state is more advantageous for tax purposes than organizing in their home state. Many companies will opt to create a Nevada or Delaware based corporation even though they may in fact have the company located in another state. This is the same situation when it comes to Church formation. A Church can be created through our Church Establishment Affidavit in one state (example: New York) but organizes their legal Corporation Sole through the State of Alaska (as long as they have a registered agent representing them in that state). We recommend applying with us because our church, The Empowerment Center Church is willing to act as the registered agent for approved churches we agree to help. Any resident of the 7 Corporate Sole states can act as your registered agent. Through common law, your home state will fully recognize your church and Corporation Sole's tax-exempt status. You will be able to open subsequent bank accounts and even online merchant accounts with your new Corporation Sole! When opening up a bank account in your state, typically the bank will require certified copies of your Articles of

Incorporation for your Corporate Sole as well as your Federal EIN number. Always remember though, it's at the discretion of the bank for what items they will require prior to opening an account. Some banks (especially credit unions) can deny you an account if you do not meet their preferences. Most of the larger banking institutions, like BofA, will open your account with nothing more than the two items described above (the Certified Articles of Incorporation and your Federal EIN number).

Do you need to have a physical church building (i.e. 4 walls and a steeple) in order to have a Corporation Sole?
Answer: NO. A church is defined as, *"In its most general sense, the religious society founded and established by Jesus Christ, to receive, preserve, and propagate His doctrines and ordinances."* – source: *Blacks Law Dictionary 5th Edition.* So, by definition, you and I as brothers and sisters in Christ, literally ARE defined as the church! Now, how do we lawfully fulfill this definition and at the same time fulfill even the IRS's own 14-point preferences for what they would like to see in a church? We do this through our Church Establishment Affidavit. It is written in such a manner that not only lawfully fulfills 26 U.S.C 508 but it also meets the preferences of the IRS's own 14-point requirements used to determine a *bona fide* church. We took months carefully researching the right verbiage that would meet every requirement (State and Federal) to have a *bona fide* church. After consultation with many federal criminal defense attorneys, we felt that our current affidavit lawfully fulfills ALL of these requirements. So, your church is technically manifested through the affidavit and NOT through a physical building structure. We structured the church's creation this way for many reasons, chiefly due to prevent any federal agency attempt to disprove your affidavit in court. Technically, the justice department and the IRS cannot disprove your affidavit in a federal courtroom or attempt to prove that you're NOT indeed a church. Doing it this way creates a significant legal boundary for the IRS and any justice department officials attempting to prove that you're in fact NOT a church by not having a physical church building for congregation members to meet in. In fact, many of today's

ministers preach online instead of having a physical church building! With developments in Internet and telecommunications, more and more ministers are opting to have webinars, conference calls and pre-recorded video sermons distributed to a larger congregation audience online rather than limiting their message to those in a brick and mortar building location within their city. Who is to say that people watching your sermons online cannot have the same spiritual experience as they could have if they physically sat in a building with you? Is an IRS official capable of making that determination? NO. This is why we added this layer of protection for you.

Is a Corporation Sole lawfully required to have a polity body or board of trustees like other 501c3's?
Answer: No. A Corporation Sole is not required by law to have either a polity body or a board of trustees.

In fact, this is reaffirmed in the Oregon law of ORS 65.067 which states,

"Any individual may, in conformity with the constitution, canons, rules, regulations and disciplines of any church or religious denomination, form a corporation hereunder to be a corporation sole. Such corporation shall be a form of religious corporation and will differ from other such corporations organized hereunder only in that it shall have no board of directors, need not have officers and shall be managed by a single director who shall be the individual constituting the corporation and its incorporator or the successor of the incorporator."

The Corporation Sole DOES have a Successor and Secretary, but not the traditional polity body or board of trustee's that govern a traditional Church and have veto power to overrule a Pastors decision to appropriate funds in any direction the Lord lays on their heart to choose.

This gives the Corporation Sole innumerable advantages over a traditional 501c3 Church.

Do you need to become an ordained minister in order to form a Corporation Sole?
Answer: YES, but not in the way you've traditionally been taught. Traditionally, a senior minister is granted a license or is ordained after completing a prescribed amount of studies through their church's denominational university. Under normal circumstances, this ordination "license" is limited to that particular denomination. It should be noted that ALL licenses and incorporations pursuant to United States Supreme Court ruling Hale v Henkle 1905 are considered "Creatures of the State" by common law. So, when a pastor calls me and states that he/she is a "licensed ordained minister", I understand that all they really just admitted too, is that under 501c3 they really are just a "creature of the state" (which in the Kingdom of God, doesn't stand for too much).

We have created a solution whereas our Church Establishment Affidavit lawfully fulfills this preference of the IRS. The IRS has what they call their 14 point "test" of preferences which they require to determine whether or not a church is a true *bona fide* church, according to their definition. Their language states that ministers should be selected only after completing a prescribed amount of studies. Our affidavit's language fulfills this preference. Take note that I said, "preference". The IRS's 14 point test to a church is not written in any law here in America. It is an internal review board's "*preference*" that you meet these standards if they are holding a formal church inquiry against you. Their rulings can also be challenged in a Federal Courtroom (whereas, in a Federal Constitutional courtroom, no jury can disprove you're NOT a church pursuant to your initially signed affidavit). So, the short answer is YES, you need to be ordained. But in this case our Church Establishment Affidavit and the people signing it are the ones ordaining you *through* that legal document.

Is the Corporate Sole a Scam?

Answer: Only if its being used for its "unintended purpose". A Corporate sole was invented to enable *bona fide* religious leaders to hold property and conduct business for the benefit of the religious entity. A Corporation Sole may own property and enter into contracts as a natural person, but only for the purposes of the religious entity and not for the individual office holder's personal benefit. Title to property that vests in the office holder as a Corporation Sole passes not to the office holder's heirs, but to the successors to the office by operation of law. A legitimate Corporation Sole is designed to ensure continuity of ownership of property dedicated to the benefit of a legitimate religious organization. Also, failure to properly establish your church prior to incorporating a Corporation Sole will deem you as being out of statutory compliance in law. One cannot simply just go incorporate a Corporation Sole and then all of a sudden think that gives them the authority to use it as a personal tax shelter *(which is NOT its intended purpose)*. In fact, anyone that would view the Corporation Sole as a glorified tax shelter, to attempt to hide lawful taxes owed, would be committing a possible felony act of attempting to defraud the Federal Government of Taxation (which is NOT a good thing). You MUST FIRST properly establish a church through the recommended *"Church Establishment Affidavit"* before EVER thinking of incorporating a Corporation Sole. You will notice that certain Corporate Sole peddlers will not try to establish the Corporation Sole properly and will go right to incorporating one without first laying down a church's foundation. These few illegitimate Corporate Sole peddlers would tarnish the reputation of legitimate *bona fide* churches Corporation Sole pastors who desire to finally be free and unshackled from the restrictive 501c3 law.

Can you have a church located in one state yet have a Corporation Sole organized in another state?
Answer: YES. This is due to us, or another registered agent, acting as your Oregon based domiciled registered agent. As with any incorporation in the United States, an organization (in this case, a church) can elect to incorporate in any state or jurisdiction. Example: Many companies throughout America

elect to incorporate their business in Nevada due to their tax laws (even though the organization is based entirely in a different state). Our Corporation Sole, "The Empowerment Center Overseers and Successors, a Corporation Sole" is willing to act as your registered agent in order to make this possible for you *(so long as your application is approved by us).* A registered agent in one of the eight states that recognize corporate sole is needed, especially if you live in one of the 43 states that don't currently have a Corporate Sole law enacted.

What qualifications should you have before getting a Corporation Sole?
Answer: This is an in-depth theological question. I try to answer it as the Holy Spirit leads me. Some people may agree, while others vehemently disagree. Since this answer is based on my personal interpretation of scripture (mainly 1st Timothy chapter 3), this should only be considered a reflection of our church, The Empowerment Center's, standard in which we personally qualify folks who have a calling to organize their church with a Corporation Sole. First, let's take a look at what 1st Timothy chapter 3 has to say regarding "overseers", it says:

"Here is a trustworthy saying: Whoever aspires to be an overseer desires a noble task. 2 Now the overseer is to be above reproach, faithful to his wife, temperate, self-controlled, respectable, hospitable, able to teach, 3 not given to drunkenness, not violent but gentle, not quarrelsome, not a lover of money. 4 He must manage his own family well and see that his children obey him, and he must do so in a manner worthy of full respect. 5 (If anyone does not know how to manage his own family, how can he take care of God's church?) 6 He must not be a recent convert, or he may become conceited and fall under the same judgment as the devil. 7 He must also have a good reputation with outsiders, so that he will not fall into disgrace and into the devil's trap.

11 In the same way, their wives are to be worthy of respect, not malicious talkers but temperate and trustworthy in everything."

If a man or woman is a recent convert or has their house completely out of Godly order, then it might be appropriate to have that person go through some form of discipleship or leadership training prior to applying for their Corporate Sole. Our standard here at The Empowerment Center is taken directly from 1st Timothy chapter 3 (specifically verses 1-7 and 11).

How much does it cost to incorporate a Corporation Sole?
Answer: If you have properly established your Church through our Church Establishment Affidavit, then we lead you to go to www.churchfreedom.org/apply (to apply for us to represent you) then we'll lead you to go through our Secretary of State, their fees range from $20-$140 to file the Corporation Sole's Articles of Incorporation. If you're opting to set one up yourself in another state, then other state fee(s) may apply. Please exercise due diligence if you're attempting to do this yourself in another state other than Oregon.

Does the Corporate Sole need to have the name of the church in its incorporated name?
Answer: Yes and No. Let me explain, I will give you an example of our own Ministry:

Our church is called "The Empowerment Center" this was established with our affidavit (as we have provided in this book) for the purposes of lawfully fulfilling 26 U.S.C § 508(c)(1)(a).

Our Corporation Sole, however, is registered as "The Empowerment Center Overseer and Successors, a Corporation Sole". It is legally required to have that really long name pursuant to state law.

Therefor, since having a Corporation Sole is limited generally to bishops and overseers for any particular church, we customarily list the name of the church followed by the word "overseer". As you can see from my example above, I, Joshua Kenny-Greenwood am acting as The Empowerment Center "overseer." So, if your church was hypothetically named, "Calvary Church", then your

Corporate Sole would be called, "Calvary Church Overseer and Successors, a Corporation Sole". In some states, they may only require the name of the office which would be, "Calvary Church Overseer"!

Will the Corporation Sole's incorporated name effect the way people can write tax-deductible checks to your church and or Ministry?
Answer: NO. People ask this question a lot because of the vast difference between the name of your church and the name of your Corporation Sole. Example: Our church is called, "The Empowerment Center", whereas, the name of our Corporation Sole is called, "The Empowerment Center Overseer and Successors, a Corporation Sole". Using our own church as an example, people can easily write us a gift, tithe or offering to, "The Empowerment Center" and our bank/credit union will happily accept it.

What if we have many subsidiaries to our ministry (*such as an outreach center*) that we would like to collect separate donations for? Will donors still be able to donate to those various ministries?
Answer: Yes. There is an easy solution to this. Simple register the subsidiary ministry as a DBA under the Corporate Sole. I will use our church as an example:

Here at The Empowerment Center, we have a ministry called, "Lawful Empowerment" that teaches Christians how to better understand the law in order to take more dominion in their lives as the scripture mandates us to do. Well, if I wanted donors to be able to send a donation directly to that ministry (separate from the main Empowerment Center itself) then I would register, The Empowerment Center Overseer and Successors and Corporation Sole" (DBA, doing business as) "Lawful Empowerment". This is a simple DBA that costs very little to register. Once you have this DBA properly registered, you can then present it to you're financial banking institution in order to create a specific account for that ministry. This way, donors can now begin to write checks and donations directly to your subordinate ministries or any integrated auxiliary of your main church.

Is a Corporation Sole required by federal law to file annual information returns?
Answer: Generally, BOTH churches and Corporation Sole's are MANDATORILY exempted from filing annual information returns with the IRS pursuant to 26 U.S.C § 6033(3)(A)(1-3) which states:

(3) Exceptions from filing
(A) Mandatory exceptions
Paragraph (1) shall not apply to—
(i) churches, *their integrated auxiliaries*, and conventions or associations of churches,
(ii) any organization (other than a private foundation, as defined in section 509 (a)) described in subparagraph (C), the gross receipts of which in each taxable year are normally not more than $5,000, or
(iii) the exclusively religious activities of any religious order.

A Corporation Sole falls under the category of being an, "*Integrated Auxiliary of a Church*".

"Integrated Auxiliary of a Church" is defined by the IRS as:

The term *integrated auxiliary of a church* refers to a class of organizations that are related to a church or convention or association of churches, but are not such organizations themselves. In general, the IRS will treat an organization that meets the following three requirements as an integrated auxiliary of a church. The organization must:

1.) Be described both as an Internal Revenue Code section 501(c)(3) organization and be a public charity under Code section 509(a)(1), (2), or (3),

2.) Be affiliated with a church or convention or association of churches, and
3.) Receive financial support primarily from internal church sources as opposed to public or governmental sources.

Men and women's organizations, seminaries, mission societies and youth groups that satisfy the first two requirements above are considered integrated auxiliaries whether or not they meet the internal support requirement.

Since the Corporation Sole is an active 501c3 and it is affiliated with a church, it technically falls under the category of a "Integrated Auxiliary of a Church". It could also even be defined as section (iii)'s "the exclusively religious activities of any religious order." Therefor, generally, the Corporation Sole has a mandatory exception from even being required to file annual information returns to the IRS. In fact, as you read the language of our affidavit you will understand why we make this claim. In any event, if your Churches Corporation Sole does own an entity and that entity is conducting nothing but business that is not related to Church activities whatsoever, then it might be wise to disclose whatever income tax liability is due to the Federal Government from the business generated income. Rule of thumb is, keep your business and Church related activities separate.

Is property held by a Corporate Sole considered tax exempt?
Answer: Generally the answer is "Yes", however, some states such as New Jersey for example, require that property being held in the custody of the Corporation Sole have an occupancy permit for the property in question in order for the state to approve its tax exemption. Raw land or an empty warehouse, for example, may not be exempt from taxation. Since every single state is different in regards to having their own unique state property tax income laws, you will need to exercise due diligence and ask your state's Department of Revenue for exactly what their protocol is for claiming a property as exempt from taxation.

If I am personally blessed with a large cash tithe of offering or any offering for that matter, can I give it to the Corporate Sole and claim it as a deduction?

Answer: This is a tricky question. First, we need to establish WHERE in fact the contribution is coming from! If the donation is coming from a taxpayer, then taxpayers are required to keep excellent records of their charitable contributions. Under the Pension Protection Act, you must keep written records of all cash donations. Your records must indicate the name of the charitable organization, the date of your contribution, and the amount of your contribution. Cancelled checks work well as a written record, since the name of the charity, the date of the gift, and the amount of the gift will all be recorded on the check. Bank statements showing a gift paid by debit card and credit card statements showing a gift paid by credit card also contain these same elements needed for your records.

Charitable organizations will often provide donors with a written letter acknowledging the gift or with a receipt for the donation. These acknowledgment letters should also be kept with your tax records. If a tax return is audited, the IRS can disallow charitable donations of $250 or more if you don't have the written acknowledgement from the charity that documents your gift. The IRS advises, "If you made more than one contribution of $250 or more, you must have either a separate acknowledgment for each or one acknowledgment that lists each contribution and the date of each contribution and shows your total contributions."

What about Non-Cash Contributions of Property(s) to the Corporation Sole?

Answer: Contributions of property(s) (other than cash) are subject to strict record keeping and substantiation rules. You must be able to substantiate the fair market value of the goods or property you donated, plus keep any written acknowledgments you receive from the charity.

1. **Fair Market Value of Contributed Property?**
   You must make an assessment of the fair market value of the property you contribute.

2. **What About Non-Cash Contributions Totaling More Than $500?**
   Answer: You must attach IRS Form 8283 to your personal income tax returns if your total non-cash contribution exceeds $500 to a Corporation Sole.

3. **Regarding Car Contributions: You MUST Have Written Acknowledgement.**
   If you contribute a car, truck, boat, airplane, or other vehicle, and the vehicle is worth more than $500, you must receive a written acknowledgement from the non-profit before you can claim a tax deduction.

4. **Non-Cash Contributions over $5,000: Must Have Written Appraisal**.
   If you contribute property worth more than $5,000, you must obtain a written appraisal of the property's fair market value.

5. **Limits on the Charitable Contribution Deduction**
   Your charitable contribution tax deduction may be limited. There are limits specific to charitable contributions, and there are general limits on itemized deductions.

50%, 30%, and 20% Limits on Charitable Contributions:
4.) Generally, you can deduct cash contributions in full up to 50% of your adjusted gross income.
5.) Generally, you can deduct property contributions in full up to 30% of your adjusted gross income.

6.) Generally, you can deduct contributions of appreciated capital gains assets in full up to 20% of your adjusted gross income.

Charitable contributions in excess of these limits can be carried over to the following tax year. The excess contributions can be carried over for a maximum of five years. NOTE: Due to recent legislation, these figures may have changed to lesser percentage amounts.

6. Non-Tax Deductible Items to Consider for the Corporation Sole:
Contributions are not tax deductible if given to any of the following:
- Political parties, political campaigns, or political action committees.
- Contributions given to individual people.
- Fees or dues paid to professional associations.
- Contributions to labor unions, chambers of commerce, or business associations.
- Contributions to for-profit schools and hospitals.
- Contributions to foreign governments.
- Fines or penalties paid to local or state governments.
- The value of your time for services rendered to a non-profit.

Is my church required to have a Federal Tax EIN number or ANY Federal Tax Identification number?
Answer: NO. In fact, since you're properly establishing your church through our custom, "Church Establishment Affidavit", *(which is neither considered an incorporation, trust, community chest fund or foundation)*, your church is completely immune from the jurisdiction of 501c3's restrictive provisions and is NOT required to obtain a Federal tax identification number.

Is the Corporate Sole Required to have an EIN?

Answer: YES. It should apply for an EIN in order to establish a proper bank account. It should be noted that the church is not applying for the EIN but rather its subsequent Corporation Sole.

If the Corporate Sole is exempted from taxation, how does our church keep up with its bookkeeping?
Answer: This is a great question! Remember as well that the Corporation Sole requires no church treasurer, church polity body or appropriations committee like a traditional 501c3 church does. The Overseer of the Corporation Sole holds any and all subsequent bank accounts and financial assets alone. In addition, remember that donors are responsible for keeping records of their tax-deductible contributions. This responsibility in record keeping is NOT the churches. As a customary gesture of goodwill, I recommend that for any donations over $500, that the donor be given a receipt of acknowledgement for their contribution. Do not feel that you are lawfully compelled to give this though. It is for the sole benefit of the taxpayer being able to deduct the contribution for their end of year federal income tax returns.

Is the Corporate Sole required to receive its tax-exempt status from the IRS?
Answer: NO. It is considered an integrated auxiliary of a church and therefor mandatorily exempted from filing an IRS form 1023 seeking official recognition of its tax-exempt status.

Can a Corporate Sole open up a bank account or an online merchant account (such as a PayPal account)?
Answer: YES and YES. Banks and even online merchants, such as PayPal, will fully recognize your Corporation Sole's status. To date, every church we have supported has been able to open up both types of accounts.

How does the law define a church?
Answer: Currently there is no Federal or State law that legally defines the word, "church". Webster's Dictionary and even

Oxford Dictionary have opposing translations. The best legal definition we have encountered to date is from Blacks Law Dictionary 5th Edition which states:

CHURCH. *"In its most general sense, the religious society founded and established by Jesus Christ, to receive, preserve, and propagate His doctrines and ordinances."*

By rights, this definition means that by simply being apart of the religious society of believers of Jesus Christ that by its very definition YOU and I as Christians ARE "The Church"! This is a great philosophical argument one might make if you were defending your church's exempt status in an official IRS inquiry or even before a federal judge. However, the question remains, how does one "lawfully" prove that they are a church? To settle this matter in statutory law, we decided to create our custom "Church Establishment Affidavit". We also direct overseers at our site ChurchFreedom.org in how to put this affidavit on public notice so that it cannot be exempted as inadmissible evidence in a federal court hearing. It cannot be understated how significant this affidavit means if your church is ever challenged via an IRS official church inquiry, audit or federal appeals hearing. Being able to produce legal evidence of your church's status helps nullify any and all arguments that would attempt to disprove that its status as a church is in question by these various authorities.

Can an individual, unbeliever or person of a different faith set up a Corporation Sole?
Answer: NO. Corporation Sole's are reserved for religious leaders of *bona fide* churches only. It is NOT for unbelievers or for people(s) of a different faith from Christianity. The reason is simple enough: You cannot have a Corporation Sole without first having a church and you cannot have a church without acknowledging Jesus Christ. This is why faiths such as Islam, Judaism, and others must seek official recognition of their tax-exempt status from the IRS as a religious organization. Legitimate churches are excluded from ever doing this.

Can a Corporation Sole receive grants?
Answer: NO. Because the Corporation Sole is not required to seek official recognition of tax exemption by the IRS pursuant to 26 U.S.C § 508(c)(1)(a) and therefor not required to file an IRS form 1023, it is thereby ineligible to apply for tax payer funded federal grants.

Can a Corporation Sole own a business?
Answer: YES. In fact, many of these businesses can be considered tax exempt pursuant to the IRS's own standards as described below:

The Internal Revenue Code contains a number of modifications, exclusions, and exceptions to unrelated business income. For example, dividends, interest, certain other investment income, royalties, certain rental income, certain income from research activities, and gains or losses from the disposition of property are excluded when computing unrelated business income for the Corporation Sole. In addition, the following activities are specifically excluded from the definition of unrelated trade or business:

1.) **Volunteer Labor**: Any trade or business is excluded in which substantially all the work is performed for the organization without compensation. Some fundraising activities, such as volunteer operated bake sales, may meet this exception.

2.) **Convenience of Members**: Any trade or business is excluded that is carried on by an organization described in section 501(c)(3) or by a governmental college or university primarily for the convenience of its members, students, patients, officers, or employees. A typical example of this is a school cafeteria.

3.) **Selling Donated Merchandise**: Any trade or business is excluded that consists of selling merchandise,

substantially all of which the organization received as gifts or contributions. Many thrift shop operations of exempt organizations would meet this exception.
Goodwill stores are a great example of this.

4.) **Bingo**: Certain bingo games are not unrelated trade or business.

Does a Corporation Sole receive discounts on postage like other non-profits?
Answer: NO. Because the Corporation Sole is not required to seek official recognition of tax exemption by the IRS pursuant to 26 U.S.C § 508(c)(1)(a) and therefor not required to file an IRS form 1023, it is thereby ineligible to apply for reduced rates on postage. Perhaps a civil rights case is in order due to these stipulations by the federal government violating a Corporate Sole's 5th Amendment right of due process (especially since the IRS considers a Corporation Sole to be a 'natural person'. A natural person and an individual are defined by Blacks Law Dictionary 9th Edition as,

Person. (Be) 1. A human being. Also termed *natural person.*

Individual, *adj.* (I5c) 1. Existing as an indivisible entity. 2. For relating to a single person or thing, as opposed to a group.

How do I know if my church is a 501c3?
Answer: Easy, if your church is currently not financially organized through a Corporation Sole and currently is either an incorporation, has sought official recognition of its tax exempt status (i.e. filed an IRS form 1023), has received an Federal EIN number (or any tax identification number), has opened up a bank account or financial trust account (incorporated or unincorporated) in the name of the church then it is considered to be solely under the jurisdiction of 501c3 and is prevented from engaging in no substantial part of the activities of which is carrying on propaganda, or otherwise attempting, to influence legislation (except as otherwise provided in subsection (h) of 26

U.S.C § 501), and which does not participate in, or intervene in (including the publishing or distributing of statements), any political campaign on behalf of (or in opposition to) any candidate for public office.

Does the government have jurisdiction over my Corporate Sole? Also, what are some legal advantages that the Corporation Sole has?
Answer: Depends. Some states such as California have Corporation Sole laws that allow for circuit court judges to have unlimited access to a Corporation Sole's books at all times. This could potentially be challenged in federal court and ruled unconstitutional due to the IRS admitting that a Corporation Sole can enter into contracts as a, "natural person". When the IRS admitted that the Corporate Sole indeed does act as a natural person, we must remember that in United States Common law (which are rulings by the Federal Supreme Court) that in 1905 during the case Hale v Henkle that Supreme Court Justice Melville Fuller stated in his judgment: *"The individual may stand upon his constitutional Rights as a citizen. He is entitled to carry on his private business in his own way. His power to contract is unlimited. He owes no such duty [to submit his books and papers for an examination] to the State, since he receives nothing therefrom, beyond the protection of his life and property. His Rights are such as existed by the law of the land [Common Law] long antecedent to the organization of the State, and can only be taken from him by due process of law, and in accordance with the Constitution. Among his Rights are a refusal to incriminate himself, and the immunity of himself and his property from arrest or seizure except under a warrant of the law. He owes nothing to the public so long as he does not trespass upon their Rights."*

A natural person and an individual are defined by Blacks Law Dictionary 9th Edition as,

Person. (Be) 1. A human being. Also termed *natural person*.

Individual, *adj.* (I5c) 1. Existing as an indivisible entity. 2. For relating to a single person or thing, as opposed to a group.

Currently, no Corporation Sole overseer has challenged this California law based on the merits outlined above.

In addition, a Corporation Sole can sue and be sued, and defend, in all courts, and places, in all matters and proceedings wherever. It can contract in the same manner and to the same extent as a natural person, for the purposes of the trust. It can also own various other forms of incorporation's as well (such as LLC's, trusts and more). Another important legal advantage of a Corporation Sole is that it can borrow money, and give promissory notes thereof, and secure the payment thereof by mortgage or other lien upon property, real or personal. It can also claim title to real property. This is especially great for possible State Property Tax Exemptions.

Depending on the legal circumstance of how a Corporation Sole accepts the contractual jurisdiction of a Government agency (such as filing IRS returns when it is generally exempted from doing so) then the Corporation Sole can inadvertently come under governmental jurisdiction. We highly recommend you pause and consider this prior to officially signing any document with the federal government.

What if our church applies for a Corporation Sole in one of the 7 States, and then that state repeals their Corporation Sole law? What happens to our Corporation Sole if or when that happens?
Answer: This is another reason why we want to urge EVERY ministry leader in America to QUICKLY organize their church structure as we explain and have them get a Corporation Sole! You see, because of the Corporation Sole's immense power and authority, the IRS has done everything in their power to influence states to repeal their Corporation Sole laws. In fact, over the last 10 years alone there originally were 15 states that had active Corporation Sole laws, now it is less with only 7 States

remaining! Once your Corporation Sole is filed with a state that still has an active Corporation Sole law, if that state repeals that law, your Corporation Sole will be fully grandfathered in and will not cease to exist.

In short, either get organized or reorganized with a Corporation Sole as fast as you can, or you run the risk of never being able to apply if the trend of states dropping the Corporation Sole laws continue at their present pace.

Does the Corporation Sole get filed like any other corporation through the Secretary of State?

Answer: YES. If you are requesting that our Corporation Sole act as your Oregon based registered agent then the Corporation Sole itself (not the church) is filed through the Oregon SOS Corporation Division's office. It is important to add that because the church is NOT being registered nor is it seeking a Federal Taxpayer Identification Number, that it is completely outside the jurisdiction of 501c3. Only the Corporation Sole is under 501c3 regulations. Good thing: On Sunday morning, I do not preach from the power and authority of our asset holdings entity (the Corporation Sole) I preach from the power and authority of the Holy Spirit and from our signed church affidavit.

Does the Church Establishment Affidavit get filed through the Secretary of State?

Answer: YES. In the current state in which we reside, it is mandatory that this document is filed with the State.

When should we open up our Corporation Sole's checking or savings accounts?

Answer: Only AFTER you've properly signed your Church Establishment Affidavit, publically registered the Corporation Sole, have received your certified copies of your Corporation Sole's Articles of Incorporation and applied for an EIN number for your Corporation Sole. Once you have completed these steps, then you should go down to your local bank and open up your Corporation Sole checking and savings account(s).

Am I required to take a "Vow of Poverty", when setting up a church or a Corporation Sole?
Answer: the short answer is NO. You're not technically required to take a vow of poverty when setting up a Corporation Sole. Taking a vow of poverty only depends on whether or not you wish to file income tax on income generated and used outside of your ministry authority as the Overseer of the Corporation Sole for your Church. Another alternative is to file an IRS form 4361. If you did want to research ways on taking a vow of poverty, please keep the following in mind:

A "vow of poverty" is described in 26 U.S.C § 1402(e)(1)(a) which states:

(e) Ministers, members of religious orders, and Christian Science practitioners
(1) **Exemption**
Subject to paragraph (2), any individual who is
  *(A) a duly ordained, commissioned, or licensed minister of a church or a member of a religious order (other than a member of a religious order who has taken a **vow of poverty** as a member of such order).*

Here is the text from paragraph (2) which the above statement is referring to:

Verification of application.
The Secretary may approve an application for an exemption filed pursuant to paragraph (1) only if the Secretary has verified that the individual applying for the exemption is aware of the grounds on which the individual may receive an exemption pursuant to this subsection and that the individual seeks exemption on such grounds. The Secretary (or the Commissioner of Social Security under an agreement with the Secretary) shall make such verification by such means as prescribed in regulations.

The exemptions the Treasury is referring to above are related to self-employment income taxes owed. So, the law of 26 U.S.C § 1402(e)(1)(a) is designed to define taxes owed (or exempted) by duly ordained, commissioned of a church or a "member" of a religious order.

Since our custom Church Establishment Affidavit includes language that directly establishes the Corporation Sole's functions and abilities to appropriate Church related financial resources to the benefit of any individual member within the Church and since we have declared a jurisdictional distinction between the office of the Corporation Sole and the office of the Senior Pastor's position within the Church, what it comes down to is the Senior Pastors personal obligations and using the alternate resources to help pay those obligations. The IRS can make the argument that those funds given to the Pastor (not the Corporation Sole) are considered income to the Pastor and thus are potentially required to be considered as income when reporting end of the year returns for the minister.

Because a minister's income is already considered exempted from FICA taxes, this leaves the potential for you to be required to pay SECA (self employment taxes) on whatever income you generate that is outside of the Church. Also, when researching the specifics of taking a vow of poverty, the IRS requests that if you wish to be exempted from SECA taxes that you fill out a form 4029.

Here is the only problem with filing out a form 4029, you need to meet ALL of the following requirements (one of which might be impossible for your Church to meet):

Eligibility requirements.

To claim this exemption from SE tax, all the following requirements must be met.
- You must file Form 4029

- As a follower of the established teachings of the sect or division, you must be conscientiously opposed to accepting benefits of any private or public insurance that makes payments for death, disability, old age, retirement, or medical care, or provides services for medical care.
- You must waive all rights to receive any social security payment or benefit and agree that no benefits or payments will be made to anyone else based on your wages and self-employment income.
- The Commissioner of Social Security must determine that:

a.) Your sect or division has the established teachings as described in (2) above,
b.) It is the practice, and has been for a substantial period of time, for members of the sect or division to provide for their dependent members in a manner that is reasonable in view of the members' general level of living, and
c.) The sect or division has existed at all times since December 31, 1950.

The last requirement of having your sect or division being existed at all times since December 31, 1950 is really the only obstacle we foresee in hurting your chances in having your IRS form 4029 being denied by the IRS. If it is denied, then you have no SECA exemption (you do have the exemption from FICA).

Like we mentioned above, if you wish to seek an alternative to the vow of poverty, you can always elect to file an alternate form 4361 with the IRS if you do not want to pay SECA tax.

Note, this is ONLY for income being generated or derived to a Pastor that is NOT directly related to Church required or related activities that are considered non-essential to the Church.

How long does it take from start to finish to completely and totally set up a Corporation Sole (from initial application to opening up all subsequent bank accounts and even PayPal accounts)?
Answer: If you have all of your church members/congregant witnesses immediately ready to sign the Church Establishment Affidavit, and you are prepared to send all your required paperwork to us and to the Oregon Secretary of States Corporations Division as instructed to you upon your application approval, then from the time you fill out our initial application at **http://www.ChurchFreedom.org/apply** to you fully setting up all your subsequent bank accounts should reasonably take less than two weeks max to get everything completely set up and operational. Generally, this time can take much longer two weeks if a Church has already been established under 501c3 rules and that Church wants to completely reorganize their ministry with a Corporation Sole. In that instance, it can take up too several weeks if not months to completely transfer everything into the custody of the newly formed Corporation Sole.

Should a checking account be established before any tithes, offerings or donations are received? Can a donor just write a donation check out to me personally until I set up the church's bank accounts?
Answer: Once your affidavit has been signed, your articles of incorporation have been sent to the Secretary of States office, after you've received a certified copy of your articles of incorporation sent directly to you and after you have successfully applied for your EIN number for your Corporation Sole, THEN you need to definitely set up your Corporation Sole's bank accounts. I recommend that you wait to receive donations

until you have completely set up your Corporation Sole and its bank accounts. If not, then you run the risk of not being able to cash or deposit the donor's check. Also, under no circumstances should you accept a donation check made out to you directly as a ministry leader. The IRS will attempt to count this as income earned on your personal income returns. Failing to report the donor's check as income on your personal federal income returns can be considered by the IRS as you falsifying a return (which is perjury) and you will be subject to possible fines, penalties and or jail time. So, DO NOT accept any checks made directly to YOU from any donor (unless you're prepared to count it as income and that the donor understands that their check is NOT tax deductible).

Are both a church and its subsequent Corporation Sole required to have by-laws?

Answer: No. In fact church "by-laws" are one of the only reasons why denominations are one of the sole sources of division among believes. By-laws create condemnation through a denominations personal "standard of holiness" preference. Though they are created from good intentions, they do nothing but bring forth condemnation for those not good enough to live up to each standard. This was the whole purpose of Christ dying on the cross! Jesus acted as the ultimate sin offering so that he could fulfill the law (Matthew 5:17) and by doing so he, *"having cancelled the written code, with its regulations, that was against us and that stood opposed to us; he took it away, nailing it to the cross. And having disarmed the powers and authorities, he made a public spectacle of them, triumphing over them by the cross"* (Colossians 2:14-15 NIV).

Jesus summed up ALL of the laws of the prophets in Matthew 22:37-40 which he clearly stated, *"Love the Lord your God with all your heart and with all your soul and with all your mind.' This is the first and greatest commandment. And the second is like it: 'Love your neighbor as yourself.' All the Law and the Prophets hang on these two commandments."*

Every other secondary, 'by-law' a church can create outside of these two great commandments is MAN MADE and not Holy Spirit inspired. This does not mean that there is not to be Godly order in the church. Far from it, the Bible clearly teaches us how we should elect leaders (1st Timothy 3) and how certain disputes among believers should be resolved (Matthew 18) or even how to resolve internal cases of sexual immorality (1st Corinthians 5). However, a church with by-laws is unique because it goes beyond biblical protocol and into subjects like "Qualifications for Membership" and other standards of holiness that inadvertently create both a spirit of religion and condemnation for those not fully living up to the standard set by this type of "by-law".

I can personally give you several examples of how treacherous these various denominational by-laws can be. I've personally attended a church that denied a man membership with a congregation simply because he drove a beer truck! Not because he drank any beer, but simply because he drove the truck and they claimed that this was against a particular by-law within that church. So, even though I watched this man diligently participate in all aspects of the church, they still denied him full membership. This did nothing but create continued condemnation for the believer. He never felt like he fully lived up to the church's standard of holiness and therefor was never fully "qualified" to receive favor from the Lord. I've been invited to certain churches where I was denied communion because I was not an approved member! Pastors of certain denominations have even told me that according to their by-laws I am not truly saved unless I was baptized in water or that I was never full of the Holy Spirit unless I spoke in tongues. I've been told that if I am not Catholic, that I am nothing more than a "protestant". These are words and laws that do absolutely nothing but divide the church. It was the entire reason why the Apostle Paul wrote passages such as Romans chapter 14 and Galatians chapter 3.

The Body of Christ is supposed to bring FREEDOM to the lost, not to put then into further bondage and condemnation!

This is another reason why a church and Corporation Sole are so vital to us; they completely free the Body of Christ from the creation of these by-laws. The Corporation Sole is one of the only ways in America that a church can lawfully organize itself and NOT be required to create official by-laws.

Can the Corporation Sole's Successor and Secretary be the same person or two different people? Also, can either my underage son or daughter be named to either of these positions as well?

Answer: Generally, if a married couple applies for a church and Corporation Sole, I always recommend that the spouse be named as BOTH the Successor and or Secretary. This allows the Corporation Sole to have a continued continuity of its office title position. Typically, if I see a married couple apply and the spouse is NOT listed as either the successor or secretary, it usually sends up red flags to me because 9 out of 10 times it has shown us that something is out of Godly order within that marriage and will need to be fixed prior to completely setting up their church. For single folks looking to start their own church and Corporation Sole, the answer is YES you may have one or even two completely separate people in charge of those two different positions. As far as underage children go, I would have to say NO. They should only be listed upon them coming to age and being able to competently and lawfully fill out an affidavit under penalty of perjury and never beforehand. If they are underage, they most likely have no spiritual, mental, emotional or educational maturity to handle such an enormous position of authority within the Body of Christ. Please take careful consideration to who you elect to these positions because they will be the future administrators of your entire ministry.

Can an Individual Person have multiple Corporation Soles?
Answer: No. In order to remain within Canon law and statutory compliance, an individual ministry leader of a bona fide church should only be an Overseer/Bishop to only ONE Corporation Sole. Understand that a Corporation Sole is typically limited to heads of dioceses. Therefore, an individual cannot simultaneously be the head of one diocese, while at the same

time attempting to operate as the head of completely different dioceses. Only in the event of a move from one state to another should it be applicable to set up a new Church Establishment Affidavit and a new Corporation Sole to reflect the new Church in the new area.

The Introduction of IRS publication 1827 States: "Churches and religious organizations may be legally organized in a variety of ways under state law, such as unincorporated associations, nonprofit corporations, corporations sole, and charitable trusts." Isn't a church that is legally established under any of these organizations subject to the 26 U.S.C § 508(c)(1)(a) exemption law?
Answer: No. The instant that unincorporated association gets an EIN, financial trust or bank account, the ENTIRE organization falls under the complete jurisdiction of 501c3. Remember that 501c3 is not just for incorporations; it is also for trusts, community chests, funds or foundations. This means that ANYTHING related to finances or banking will automatically bring the entire ministry under the covering of 501c3. The Corporation Sole is the only known entity to allow for a true separation of a church's banking accounts and the church itself (which is manifested through our unincorporated Church Establishment Affidavit).

How does a Corporation Sole protect a church any differently from all 501c3 stipulations (such as political lobbying)? It seems to be that a church (no matter how it is legally formed) is still subject to all qualifications and disqualifications of the 501c3 law.
Answer: Remember, the Corporation Sole is NOT your church! The church your creating is a COMPLETELY separate legal entity formed via our Church Establishment Affidavit and is therefor under the jurisdiction of 26 U.S.C 508(c)(1)(a) which unlike 501c3 has NO CONDITIONS to the privilege of it's MANDATORY tax exemption.

2 Documents
* *w/ EIN*
* *w/o EIN*

CALIFORNIA Corporation Sole regulation (10009) stipulates that "Any judge of the superior court in the county in which a corporation sole has its principal office shall at all times have access to the books of the corporation." If I establish a Corporation Sole through Oregon, but still have my principal office in California, aren't my books still accessible by the Superior Court in the county where my principal office is?
Answer: No. This is because that California law is only in relationship to Corporation Soles registered contractually through the State of California. California has no jurisdiction to either dissolve or enforce its laws on a Corporation Sole organized in a different state and jurisdiction.

If I am not trying to hide behind a "tax shelter" or get out of paying "unrelated business entity taxes" then why should it matter if my books are available to a Superior Court – IF both myself and my members and contributors have followed the stipulations regarding "donations and contributions" outlined for Corporations by the Secretary of State and by the IRS Tax Codes Sections 501-508?
Answer: It matters for EVERYTHING the Corporation Sole protects and establishes! The Government should NEVER in a million years have jurisdiction over the sovereign church. The church was NEVER intended to become a "creature of the state" but rather to be a creature under headship of Jesus Christ Himself. If any pastor we know has no philosophical problems whatsoever with the government having any jurisdiction over their ministry, we would tell them to go get a *"non-profit religious organization"* like the rest of the 99% of other ministries are organized in this country. Under Malachi 3, those finances given to the church belong solely to the Lord and are

simply managed by us leaders as His stewards. Our church and Corporation Sole will have no part of, nor support whatsoever, any pastor that holds to the position that it is acceptable for ANY portion of the government to have jurisdiction over ANYTHING related to a sovereign church.

What's the legal definition of a Corporation Sole?
Answer: According to Blacks Law Dictionary 9th Edition, the word Corporation Sole is defined as:

Corporation Sole: *A series of successive persons holding an office; a continuous legal personality that is attributed to successive holders of certain monarchical or ecclesiastical positions, such as kings, bishops, rectors, vicars, and the like. This continuous personality is viewed, by legal fiction, as having the qualities of a corporation.*

When signing legal documents on behalf of my ministry's Corporation Sole, do I need to use my personal signature or sign in the name of the Corporation Sole itself?
Answer: When conducting Church business as the Corporation Sole, DO NOT USE your personal signature but rather that of the Corporation Sole. Example: Instead of writing on a Corporation Sole check, Joshua Kenny-Greenwood, I would instead write: The Empowerment Center Overseer and Successors, a Corporation Sole. This is VERY IMPORTANT to remember especially in matters related to real estate transactions or title transfer actions because a Corporation Sole acts a *Natural Person* in ALL Church business related matters.

Can a Corporation Sole issue Promissory Notes?
Answer: Yes, a Corporation Sole can issue promissory notes. A Promissory note is defined by Blacks Law Dictionary 9th Edition as:

promissory note. *(18c) An unconditional written promise, signed by the maker, to pay absolutely and in any event a certain sum of* *money either to, or to the order of, the bearer or a designated person.*

Since we are the Temple of the Holy Ghost, would that not make us automatically tax exempt at our conversion and confirmed by our baptismal record?

Answer: This is a great philosophical question since the word Church is described as, *"In its most general sense, the religious society founded and established by Jesus Christ, to receive, preserve, and propagate His doctrines and ordinances." –source: Blacks Law Dictionary 5th Edition.* This means, that if you are a Christian, then by literal definition you ARE the Church. Since the word 'Church' is described as mandatorily tax exempted in 26 USC 508(c)(1)(a), one could potentially come up with a creative conclusion that YOU (personally) are exempted from taxation. This is a great philosophical argument and is probably more creative than it is persuasive. You would probably ending up getting laughed out of Federal Court if you used that argument to evade paying lawful taxes owed to the Federal Government. Therefor, I would not recommend using this argument to avoid paying or avoid filing tax returns for your personal individual income.

Is the Corporation Sole Considered Either a Church or a Ministry?

Answer: NO. The Corporation Sole is nothing more than an office held within the Church that acts as a natural person to manage all of the Churches financial assets and business dealings.

Is there a reason why the ALL CAPS names are used when signing our Affidavit? Doesn't a name in ALL CAPITAL LETTERS signify the government created, "Strawman"?

Answer: The spelling of a name in ALL CAPS is relevant via the UCC's conspicuous clause (See http://www.law.cornell.edu/ucc/1/1-201). Not a single "guru" has ANY lawful merit whatsoever to make the assertion that your name being in ALL CAPS signifies that you are a "corporate man" or "straw man". In fact, the FBI has a warning about this theory here: http://www.fbi.gov/stats-services/publications/law-enforcement-bulletin/september-2011/sovereign-citizens.

I made sure to do a TON of homework on this topic because we had a teacher that helped with our lawful empowerment once that attempted to teach on this topic. In order to fact check his assertions I began reviewing case laws (just like I did with the Corporation Sole before writing the book) and found that his claims of ALL CAPS and the Strawman have already been attempted in Federal Court multiple times and each time it was utterly dismissed.

Now, let me reference some common law rulings that these "gurus" conveniently leave out of their presentations:

Russell v. US (WD Mich 1997) 969 F.Supp 24. "Petitioner...claims because his name is in all capital letters on the summons, he is not subject to the summons...completely without merit, patently frivolous, and will be rejected without expending any more of this court's resources."

Gdowik v. US (Bankr. SD Fla unpub 7/23/96) 78 AFTR2d 6243 aff'd (SD Fla unpub 11/6/97) 228 Bankr.Rptr 481, 482 80 AFTR2d 8254. Claims that "the use of his name JOHN E GDOWIK is an 'illegal misnomer' and use of said name violates the right to his "lawful status" was rejected.

US v. Washington (SDNY 1996) 947 F.Supp 87. "Finally, the defendant contends that the indictment must be dismissed because 'Kurt Washington,' spelled out in capital letters, is a fictitious name used by the Government to tax him improperly as a business, and that the correct spelling and presentation of his name is 'Kurt Washington.' This contention is baseless."

Rippy v. IRS (ND Calif unpub 1/26/99). "Plaintiff's response...consists of nothing more than a protest against the capitalization of his name in the caption. Accordingly, summary judgment is granted in favor of defendants and against plaintiff." The same ruling is in Hancock v. State of Utah (10th Cir unpub 5/10/99) 176 F3d 488(t).

US v. M.L. Lindsay (10th Cir 7/1/99) F3d, 99 USTC para 50648, 84 AFTR2d 5102. Tax evasion defendant's refusal to read court papers that capitalized his name and his other misbehavior justified the court refusing to reduce his sentence.

Stoecklin v. US (MD Fla unpub 12/8/97). "Tax evader complained of his name being in a prior order issued by this court and then...makes and incorrect reference to this form of using all capital letters as being proper only in reference to corporate entities. This is an incorrect statement of the law...is illustrative of [his] continued harassing and frivolous behavior."

Boyce v. CIR (9/25/96) TC Memo 1996-439 aff'd (9th Cir 1997) 122 F3d 1069. An objection to the spelling of petitioners' names in capital letters because they are not 'fictitious entities'" was rejected.

US v. Lindbloom (WD Wash unpub 4/16/97) 79 AFTR 2d 2578, 97 USTC para 50650. "In this submission, Mr. Lindbloom states that he and his wife are not proper defendants to this action because their names are not spelled with all capital letters as indicated in the civil caption." The CAPS argument and the "refused for fraud" contention were rejected.

Does the Corporation Sole Receive a Tax Exempt ID number from the IRS?

Answer: Yes. You're Corporation Sole's tax exempt ID number issued from the IRS will be the EIN number that you apply for once you've received the certified copies of your articles of incorporation for your corporation sole. It's important to note, that this tax exemption identification number WILL NOT be for your church but rather for the corporation sole itself.

Can a Corporation Sole Issue a Receipt for any Tithe or Donation that a donor can use for tax write-off?
Answer: The short answer is YES. Remember though, that donors are responsible for keeping records of their tax-deductible contributions. This responsibility in record keeping is NOT the churches nor Corporation Sole's responsibility. Traditionally however, (as a gesture of goodwill) we would recommend that for any donations over $500, that the donor be given a receipt of acknowledgement for their contribution. Do not feel that you are lawfully compelled to give this receipt though. It is for the sole benefit of the taxpayer being able to deduct the contribution for their end of year federal income tax returns and it is ultimately the responsibility of the donor to keep their records, receipts and canceled checks ready in the event of an examination by the IRS if they claim any religious deductions on their end of year returns to the IRS. Also, in order to provide participating Churches in our Corporation Sole ministry with complete excellence, we have provided each participating Overseer access to our exclusive Church, "Asset protection package" that includes access to a unique "receipt of acknowledgment" that you may give donors that they can use to write off the donation on their end of the year tax returns.

Our church takes in voluntary contributions on a monthly basis of less than $500 a month, the fact that our monthly voluntary contributions intake is so minimal, in your opinion is it just as imperative and advantageous to take the steps necessary to terminate our 501c(3) and move into a corporation sole?
Answer: Yes. Regardless of how many donations your ministry receives, it should never be entirely incorporated and considered a "Creature of the State" - pursuant to Hale v Henkle. Anytime a Church incorporates, it ceases ben being considered a Church and also rescinds its 26 USC 508(c)(1)(a) status.

Would like to understand better how a corporation sole can use three separate individuals in its governing structure. I understand that your incorporating an office and let's say the lead minister holds that office, can you still have a separate individual NOT related to you, as a secretary, even a third individual as an additional director if we choose to do so?

Answer: Great question! The Corporation Sole functions with only one SOLE individual (whom is the Overseer of the Church). It does not operate like a traditional 501c3 with 3 directors like your referring too. This is one of its benefits that makes the Corporation Sole so unique. Here is the traditional structure of the Corporation Sole:

Corporation Sole Overseer: This is typically the leader of the Church or congregant body.

Secretary: The Corporate Sole's Secretary is responsible for the efficient administration of the incorporation, particularly with regard to ensuring compliance with statutory and regulatory requirements and for ensuring that decisions by you as the sole director are implemented.

Successor: The role of the Corporate Sole's Successor is VERY IMPORTANT for several reasons. Mainly, if the primary 'Overseer' of the Corporation Sole either dies or resigns, then ALL Bank Accounts, Stocks/Bonds, Trusts, Agreements, Land Holdings, Titles, Responsibilities and EVERYTHING immediately transfer to the Successor. For all intents and purposes, the Title and Role of 'Overseer/Bishop' are instantly transferred to the Successor in either of these instances. This is a vital position and one that is typically filled by a spouse or someone that is rightfully next in line of succession in inheriting the Title of

Office in which you are creating. That's it! No other roles play a factor in the function of the Corporation Sole.

How to obtain an EIN for a Corporation Sole?
Answer: Once you get the Certified Copy of your Articles of Incorporation back from whichever state your incorporating the Corporation Sole in, you will need to go online and get an IRS EIN number for your Corporation Sole (which takes all of 3 minutes). To do this, simply go to the IRS's website and apply for a EIN number. When you finally get to the proper EIN application page, you will want to select, "View Additional Types, Including Tax-Exempt and Governmental Organizations". This will be a "Church Controlled Organization" for "Banking Purposes" only. Then you will need to select "INDIVIDUAL" and input your name, SSI and address for mailing notices. Once completed, you will be issued the EIN number. *NOTE: You will NOT be getting the EIN for your Church but rather for its subsequent Corporation Sole.

Can a Corporation Sole Issue a Receipt for any Tithe or Donation that a donor can use for tax write-off?
Answer: The short answer is YES. Remember though, that donors are responsible for keeping records of their tax-deductible contributions. This responsibility in record keeping is neither the churches nor Corporation Sole's responsibility. Traditionally however, *(as a gesture of goodwill)* we would recommend that for any donations over $500, that the donor be given a receipt of acknowledgement for their contribution. Do not feel that you are lawfully compelled to give this receipt though. It is for the sole benefit of the taxpayer being able to deduct the contribution for their end of year federal income tax returns and it is ultimately the responsibility of the donor to keep their records, receipts and canceled checks ready in the event of an examination by the IRS if they claim any religious deductions on their end of year returns to the IRS.

If I was the overseer and my spouse as the successor and secretary pass away who will then own the church and the corporation sole?
Answer: Firstly, no one "owns" the Church nor its Corporation Sole (only Yeshua Ha-Mashiach (aka, Jesus) can make that claim. If you do not have other successors in any sequential order, then those assets would be dissolved due to no leaders being present.

Is there an age requirement for opening a corporation sole? I have a son or daughter that is in their twenties.
Answer: There is no age limit requirement for someone to become an ordained minister, but I would be greatly interested in understanding how you believe your son or daughter is eligible to become an Overseer as described in 1st Timothy 3:1-13 at such a young age. I have yet to meet qualified individuals at that age to serve in this role (it's not impossible, it's just VERY rare). You would need to seriously justify his/her calling, or else the IRS would be under the impression that you're just trying to set up a tax shelter for your children. (Which could result in you BOTH ending up in Federal Prison if that was the case).

Describe the IRS and Courts 14 Point Test and How does the Affidavit lawfully fulfill these points?

We have found that the most lawful way to organize a Church before setting up it's subsequent Corporation Sole is to establish it through a legal document called a, "Church Establishment Affidavit" (which is included in this book). This affidavit serves to lawfully DECLARE and FULFILL ALL 14 points to the IRS's own definitions and standards to be considered a Church. You see, in order for a Church to meet the IRS's 14-point standards for being considered a Church, a Church must meet the following conditions:

1. Distinct legal existence

14 Points of a church (handwritten margin note)

2. Recognized creed and form of worship
3. Definite and distinct ecclesiastical government
4. Formal code of doctrine and discipline
5. Distinct religious history
6. Membership not associated with any other church or denomination
7. Organization of ordained ministers
8. Ordained ministers selected after completing prescribed courses of studies
9. Literature of its own
10. Established places of worship
11. Regular congregations
12. Regular religious services
13. Sunday schools for religious instruction of the young
14. Schools for preparation of its ministers

As you will read further in this book (by reading our affidavit), our custom Church Establishment Affidavit lawfully fulfills ALL of these various 14 points.

We already have an EIN number because we established a checking account. We have it in one city but about to plant the church in another city. Would we just give the state a change of address for the EIN number, how does that work?

ANSWER: You will NOT be using that EIN you created (in fact, we wish you would not have done that at all). Everything official will be done solely in the name of the Corporation Sole (as this book thoroughly explains). EIN, address information, articles of incorporation and etc will ALL be done NOT in the name of your Church but rather your churches subsequent Corporation Sole.

Once you make it to the password protected area of our website, you will be given specific ministry instructions for how to proceed. Simply read the book and then carefully follow Steps #1 through #3 in sequential order. DO NOT DEVIATE from our ministry instructions.

With the states trying to do away with Corporate Soles, what is the status of Oregon state. Since in Missouri we would have to go through you, therefore if Oregon followed suit would we lose it or would we be grandfathered in it. With the states trying to do away with Corporate Soles, what is the status of Oregon state. Since in Missouri we would have to go through you, therefore if Oregon followed suit would we lose it or would we be grandfathered in it.

ANSWER: I know it sounds cheesy when spoken but when I say that time is of the essence, I am not joking when it comes to the Corporation Sole. Nearly 25 years ago almost ALL 50 States had active Corporation Sole laws. Ten years ago that number went down to 16 states having the Corporation Sole law, today no more than 7 States are left standing that have an active Corporation Sole law. They literally repealed the law in Oregon because of the work of our Church there. We anticipate that at the current pace of states rescinding their current Corporation Sole laws, barring a legislative miracle, that within 5-7 years we might see the end of the modern Corporation Sole law here in America. Only those Christian Leaders that got in <u>RIGHT NOW</u> would be Grandfathered in and have the ALL the rights and benefits the Corporation Sole brings to ministries. If your Corporation Sole is set up now and is grandfathered in, your rights will never cease even if they rescind the law in its current form. This is also another reason we are trying to spread the word about ChurchFreedom.org as much as we can. God told me that, "time was of the essence" when he commanded me to write the Book on the Corporation Sole. Pray and agree that he elevates us in such a manner that we can deliver this message to tens of millions of Americans.

Does a Minister that has a Corporation Sole give themselves a Ministers Stipend Salary AND Do we pay personal income tax for any income received from the Corporation Sole?

Answer: To get the best answer, lets rely on exactly what does the IRS have to say about this topic:

Self-Employment Tax: Exemption
Ministerial services are covered by social security and Medicare provisions under the Self Employment Contributions Act (SECA). Earnings for these services are subject to self-employment tax unless one of the following applies under IRC § 1402(e):
- The minister is a member of a religious order whose members have taken a vow of poverty, or
- The minister has requested, and the IRS has approved, an exemption from self-employment tax, or
- The minister is subject only to the social security laws of a foreign country under the provisions of a social security agreement between the United States and that country (see Publication 54 for more information)

To claim exemption from self-employment tax, a minister must:
- Be an ordained, commissioned, or licensed minister of a church or denomination. Treas. Reg.§ 1.1402(c)-5
- File Form 4361. This is an application for exemption from self-employment tax for use by ministers, members of religious orders, and Christian Science practitioners. Treas. Reg. § 1.1402(e)-2A(a)(1).
- Be conscientiously opposed to public insurance (Medicare/Medicaid and Social Security benefits) because of religious beliefs. Treas. Reg. § 1.402(e)-2A(a)(2).
- File for exemption for reasons other than economic
- Notify the church or order that he or she is opposed to public insurance. Treas. Reg. § 1.402(e)-5A(b).
- Establish that the organization that ordained, licensed, or commissioned the minister is a tax-exempt religious organization.

- Establish that the organization is a church or a convention or association of churches.

Form 4361 must be filed by the due date of the Form 1040 (including extensions) for the second tax year in which at least $400 in self-employment ministerial earnings was received. The 2 years do not have to be consecutive.

An approved Form 4361 is effective for all tax years after 1967 for which a minister received $400 or more of self-employed income for ministerial services.

The exemption from self-employment tax applies only to services performed as a minister. The exemption does not apply to other self-employment income.

To determine if a minister is exempt from self-employment tax, request that he or she furnish a copy of the approved Form 4361 if it is not attached to the return. If the taxpayer cannot provide a copy, order a transcript for the year under examination. The ADP and IDRS Information handbook shows where the ministers' self-employment exemption codes are located on the transcripts and what the codes mean. Transcripts will not show exemption status prior to 1988.

If the transcript does not show a MIN SE indicator and the taxpayer still claims that he or she is exempt from self-employment tax, the Taxpayer Relations Branch at the Service Center where the Form 4361 was filed can research this information and provide the taxpayer with a copy. The Social Security Administration in Baltimore also can provide the information on exemption for an individual.

Basically, all this was saying, was that in order for you to be immune to self employment tax, you need to do a few things:

1. Be an ordained, commissioned, or licensed minister of a church or denomination. Treas. Reg.§ 1.1402(c)-5
2. File Form 4361. This is an application for exemption from self-employment tax for use by ministers, members of religious orders, and Christian Science practitioners. Treas. Reg. § 1.1402(e)-2A(a)(1).
3. Be conscientiously opposed to public insurance (Medicare/Medicaid and Social Security benefits) because of religious beliefs. Treas. Reg. § 1.402(e)-2A(a)(2).
4. File for exemption for reasons other than economic
5. Notify the church or order that he or she is opposed to public insurance. Treas. Reg. § 1.402(e)-5A(b).
6. Establish that the organization that ordained, licensed, or commissioned the minister is a tax-exempt religious organization.
7. Establish that the organization is a church or convention or association of churches.

And this needed to be done within the first two years of your new Corporation Sole's creation.

Understand, this only applies in the scenario when your doing ministry full time and the Corporation Sole is your only source of funds for taking care of the essential necessities of life and you needed to pay bills that are in your personal name but not in the Corporation Sole's, if that is the case, then those bills being paid in your name (where the Corporation Sole does not have the controlling interest) then those things in your name can be scrutinized by the Federal Government as personal income. We recommend that you consult with a CPA or Tax Professional that will help personally guide you through whatever scenario you are walking through. See from them, if you should fulfill all of the requirements listed above or if you should just count those appropriated resources from the Corporation Sole as income. At the end of the day, they will know your situation better than us to answer that question.

How Would I as a Senior Pastor to Our Church Compute Self-Employment Tax if we do not apply or seek a Self Employment Tax Exemptions

Answer: If an exemption from self-employment tax is not applied for, or is not granted, self-employment tax must be computed on ministerial earnings. To compute self-employment tax, allowable trade or business expenses are subtracted from gross ministerial earnings, then the appropriate rate is applied.

Include the following items in gross income for self-employment tax:

- Salaries and fees for services, including offerings and honoraria received for marriages, funerals, baptisms, etc.. Include gifts which are considered income as discussed under the section on income.
- Any housing allowance or utility allowances.
- Fair Rental Value (FRV) of a parsonage, if provided, including the cost of utilities and furnishings provided.
- Any amounts received for business expenses treated as paid under a nonaccountable plan, such as an auto allowance.
- Income tax or self-employment tax obligation of the minister which is paid by the Church.

Example 1

M receives a salary from the church of $20,000. His parsonage/housing allowance is $12,000. The church withholds Federal income tax (by mutual agreement) and issues him a Form W-2. He has unreimbursed employee business expenses (before excluding nondeductible amounts attributable to his exempt income) of $5,200. His net earnings for self-employment tax are $26,800 ($20,000 + $12,000 - $5,200). Note that all of M's unreimbursed business expenses are deductible for self-employment tax purposes, although the portion attributable to the exempt housing allowance is not deductible for Federal income tax purposes. IRC § 265 regarding the allocation of

99

business expenses related to exempt income relates to income tax computations but not self-employment tax computations.

Example 2
G, as shown in Example 8, computes her self-employment taxable income as follows: $12,000 salary plus $9,000 housing allowance plus $3,000 Schedule C income less ($4,500) total business expenses equals $19,500 self-employment income.
NOTE: IRS Publication 517, Social Security and Other Information for Members of the Clergy and Religious Workers is a very useful guide for taxpayers and as a quick reference.

Source for this answer: IRS Minister Audit Technique Guide Publication date - April 2009.

Should a Church pay its staff an Employee's or Independent Contractors?

Answer: A minister can be a common law employee for income tax purposes even though the payments for services as a minister is statutorily considered income from self employment for social security and medical taxes and the minister can even apply to be exempt from social security tax.

The handling of business expenses for income tax purposes is determined by whether the minister is classified as an employee or an independent contractor. If an independent contractor then the business expenses are reported on the Schedule C. If an employee then the expenses are reportable subject to statutory limitations as an employee business expense itemized deduction. To be properly reported on Schedule C, a minister's expense must come from a trade or business of his own, other than that of being an employee.

The fundamental question of employee vs. independent contractor status has received extensive statutory, regulatory, and judicial attention. The statute defines an employee as one who is such "under the usual common law rules applicable in

determining the employer-employee relationship...." IRC § 3121(d)(2). See also Treas. Reg. § 31.3121(d)-1(c).
This subject is complex and dependent on the facts and circumstances in each case, which is why it is highly litigated. As follows is a brief discussion of the subject. Research should be conducted on litigation that has occurred in your appeals circuit to assist in making the status determination. The litigation has generally occurred where the minister claims independent contractor status and the Internal Revenue Service determines the minister was an employee.

The Internal Revenue Services looks at factors that fall within three categories, namely behavioral control, financial control and the relationships of the parties. Behavioral control deals with facts that substantiate the right to direct or control the detail and means by which a worker performs the required services. Financial control deals with facts of the economic aspects of the relationship of the parties and if the worker has the opportunity for the realization of profit or loss. Some factors are: significant investment, un-reimbursed expenses, making services available, and methods of payments. Relationship of the parties is important because it reflects the parties' intent concerning control.

The Courts consider various factors to determine an employment relationship between the parties. Relevant factors include:

- The degree of control exercised by the principal over the details of the work;
- Which party invests in the facilities used in the work;
- The opportunity of the individual for profit or loss;
- Whether or not the principal has the right to discharge the individual;
- Whether the work is part of the principal's regular business;
- The permanency of the relationship; and
- Relationship the parties believe they are creating.

No one factor dictates the outcome. Rather, we must look at all the facts and circumstances of each case. *Weber v. Commissioner*, 60 F.3rd 1104, 1110 (4th Cir. 1995)
In the *Weber* case, where the issue was whether a minister was an employee or independent contractor, the court stated:

"The "right-to-control" test is the crucial test to determine the nature of the working relationship...The degree of control is one of great importance, though not exclusive...Accordingly, we must examine not only the control exercised by the alleged employer, but also the degree to which an alleged employer may intervene to imposed control...In order for an employer to retain the requisite control over the details of an employee's work, the employer need not stand over the employee and direct every move made by that employee...Also, the degree of control necessary to find employee status varies according to the nature of the services provided...The threshold level of control necessary to find employee status is generally lower when applied to professional services than when applied to nonprofessional services...In *James v. Commissioner* 25 T.C. 1296 (1956), this Court stated that "despite this absence of direct control over the manner in which professional men (and women) shall conduct their professional activities, it cannot be doubted that many professional men (and women) are employees". Also in *Azad v. United States*, 388 F.2d 74 (8th Circuit, 1968), the Court of Appeals for the Eight Circuit said that "From the very nature of the services rendered by *** professionals, it would be wholly unrealistic to suggest that an employer should undertake the task of controlling the manner in which the professional conducts his activities" Generally a lower level of control applies to professional."

The absence of the need to control the manner in which the minister conducts his or her duties should not be confused with the absence of the right to control. The right to control contemplated by the common law as an incident of employment requires only such supervision as the nature of the work requires. *McGuire v. United States*, 349 F.2d 644, 646 (9th Circuit 1965).

Finally, section 530 of the Revenue Act of 1978 does not apply to the minister's status since they are statutorily exempt from FICA and are subject to SECA. The employer has no federal employment tax obligations. Section 530 terminates the business's, but not the worker's, employment tax liability.

Exhibit 1 JOB AID
Exclusion of Parsonage Allowance under Internal Revenue Code § 107
Home Owned Or Rented/ Housing Allowance Received
The exclusion is limited to the least of:

1. Amount designated as housing allowance

2. Amount actually used to provide a home which is composed of the following items:
   - Rent
   - House payments
   - Furnishing
   - Repairs
   - Insurance, Taxes
   - Utilities
   - Other Expenses

3. Fair rental value of home, including furniture, utilities, garage
Amount excludible from income tax liability is the least of 1,2, or 3 above.

If Parsonage provided, you can deduct only the fair rental value

The entire designated housing allowance is subject to self-employment tax unless you have been approved for exemption or are retired.

Exhibit 2 Job Aid
Computation of Allowable Expenses When Tax-Exempt Income Is Received

Step 1 Enter amount of tax-exempt income (Housing allowance or fair rental value of parsonage provided)

Step 2 Total income from ministry computed by adding the following:
- Salary
- Fees
- Allowances
- Step 1 Amount

Step 2 Total of items above to derive total income from ministry

Step 3: Divide step 1 amount by total step 2 amount to obtain the non taxable income %

Step 4 Compute total business expenses substantiated by adding the following items
- Auto
- Travel
- M & E
- Other

Step 4 total of items above to derive total business expenses substantiated

Step 5 Multiply step 4 total by step 3 percentage to obtain nondeductible expenses allocable to tax exempt income

Step 6 Subtract step 5 amount from step 4 amount to obtain the deductible expenses for Federal Income tax purposes

Source for this answer: IRS Minister Audit Technique Guide Publication date - April 2009.

What Income Should Be Reported to the IRS as Income Generated from Either the Church or The Corporation Sole?

Answer:

We included this question and it's answer (directly from the IRS's own materials) because many Churches we help are larger and have multiple sources of income and or have multiple employees. Because the Church holds multiple offices (such as the Senior Pastor and Overseer) positions, it is important that if the IRS ever audited you, that you had every piece of knowledge at your disposal to better understand how to file your personal returns at the end of the year.

Income Issues:

Audit techniques required are in IRM 4.10.4 and summarized on the Examiner's Mandatory Lead Sheet Work Paper #400 "Minimum Income Probe Lead Sheet". The following provides information specific to this industry to assist in performing the various income analyses. (Note: Under IRC § 7602(e), the Service may not use indirect methods to reconstruct income unless it "has a reasonable indication that there is a likelihood of...unreported income." See IRM 4.10.4 for the techniques that should be employed to determine whether there is a likelihood of unreported income.)

Income To Be Reported

A minister usually receives compensation from the employing church or church agency for personal services but may also receive bonuses or "special gifts." In addition, the minister may receive fees paid directly from parishioners for performing weddings, funerals, baptisms, masses and other contributions received for services. Under Treas. Reg. § 1.61-2(a)(1), all are includible in gross income, along with expense allowances for travel, transportation, or other business expenses received under a nonaccountable plan. If the church or church agency

105

pays amounts in addition to salary to cover the minister's self-employment tax or income tax, these are also includible in gross income. Rev. Rul. 68-507, 1968-2 C.B. 485.

Fees for weddings, funerals, etc., given directly to the church rather than to the minister are not considered compensation to the minister. Contributions made to or for the support of individual missionaries to further the objectives of their missions are includible in gross income. Rev. Rul. 68-67, 1968-1 C.B. 38.

A minister's compensation package often includes a designated parsonage allowance, that is, the use of church owned housing, a housing allowance, or a rental allowance. This is treated differently for income tax and self-employment tax purposes, and is discussed in detail below in the section on Parsonage allowance.

Gift or Compensation for Services

You need to look at the facts and circumstances of each transfer. Some transfers are obvious gifts while others might actually be compensation for services.

IRC § 61(a) provides that gross income includes all income from whatever source derived unless specifically excluded by the Code. Compensation for services in whatever form received is definitely included in income. IRC § 102(a) excluded from gross income the value of property acquired by gift. Whether an item is a gift is a factual question and the taxpayer bears the burden of proof. The most significant fact is the intention of the taxpayer. The Supreme Court provided guidance in this area in two key cases which were summarized in *Charles E Banks and Rose M Banks v. Commissioner*, T.C. Memo. 1991-641 as follows:

"In *Commissioner v. Duberstein*, 363 U.S. 278, 4 L. Ed. 2d 1218, 80 S. Ct. 1190 (1960); at 285-286, the Supreme Court stated the governing principles in this area: the mere absence of a legal or

moral obligation to make such a payment does not establish that it is a gift. And, importantly, if the payment proceeds primarily from "the constraining force of any moral or legal duty," or from "the incentive of anticipated benefit" of an economic nature, it is not a gift. And, conversely, "where the payment is in return for services rendered, it is irrelevant that the donor derives no economic benefit from it." A gift in the statutory sense, on the other hand, proceeds from a "detached and disinterested generosity," "out of affection, respect, admiration, charity or like impulses." And in this regard, the most critical consideration, is the transferor's "intention." "What controls is the intention with which payment, however voluntary, has been made."
The intention of the transferor is a question of fact to be determined by "the application of the fact-finding tribunal's experience with the mainsprings of human conduct to the totality of the facts of each case." *Commissioner v. Duberstein*, supra at 289.

We must make an objective inquiry into the circumstances surrounding the transfer rather than relying on the transferor's subjective characterization of the transfer. *Commissioner v. Duberstein*, supra at 286; *Bogardus v. Commissioner*, 302 U.S. 34, 43 (1937).

In the *Charles E Banks and Rose M Banks v. Commissioner*, T.C. Memo. 1991-641, case a structured and organized transfer of cash from members of the church took place on four special days of each year. Prior to making the transfers, members of the Church met amongst themselves to discuss the transfers. The amounts of the transfers were significant. Several members testified in Court. Their testimony indicated "the primary reason for the transfers at issue was not detached and disinterested generosity, but rather, the church members' desire to reward petitioner for her services as a pastor and their desire that she remain in that capacity." The Court ruled the transfers were compensation for services hence included in gross income.
In *Lloyd L. Goodwin v. U.S.*, 870 F. Supp 265, 269 (S.D. Iowa 1994), aff'd 67 F. 3d 149 (8th Cir. 1995), a similar situation

existed. Cash was collected from the congregation as a whole on established special occasion days. The collection was done by the congregation leaders in a structured manner. The fact was revealed that the congregation knew that it probably could not retain the pastor's service at his relatively low salary without the additional payments. The Court ruled the funds as compensation for services, not gifts.

There are numerous court cases that ruled the organized authorization of funds to be paid to a retired minister at or near the time of retirement were gifts and not compensation for past services. Rev. Rul. 55-422, 1955-1 C.B. 14, discusses the fact pattern of those cases which would render the payments as gifts and not compensation.

The Tax Court had ruled in *Potito v. Commissioner*, T.C. Memo 1975-187, aff'd 534 F2d 49 (5th Cir. 1976), that the value of a boat, motor and boat trailer was included in gross income as payment for services. The taxpayer, a minister, had not produced any evidence regarding the intention of the donors that the transfer of the property was out of "detached and disinterested generosity".

The Parsonage Allowance

IRC § 107 provides an exclusion from gross income for a "parsonage allowance," housing specifically provided as part of the compensation for the services performed as a minister of the gospel. This includes the rental value of a home furnished to him or her as part of compensation or a housing allowance, to the extent that the payment is used to rent or provide a home and to the extent such allowance does not exceed the fair rental value (FRV) of the home, including furnishings and appurtenances such as a garage and the cost of utilities. IRC § 107(2). The term "parsonage allowance" includes church provided parsonages, rental allowances with which the minister may rent a home and housing allowances with which the minister may purchase a home. A minister can receive a parsonage allowance for only one home.

A housing allowance must be included in the minister's gross income in the taxable year in which it is received to the extent that such allowance is not used by him during the taxable year to rent or otherwise provide a home or exceeds the FRV of the home including furnishings and appurtenances such as a garage and the cost of utilities. Treas. Reg. § 1.107-1(c) and IRC § 107(2). The value of the "allowed" parsonage allowance is not included in computing the minister's income subject to income tax and should not be included in W-2 wages. However, the parsonage allowance is subject to self-employment tax along with other earnings. IRC § 1402(a)(8). (See special rules for retired ministers below). If a church-owned parsonage is provided to the minister, instead of a housing allowance, the fair rental value of the housing must be determined. Determining the fair rental value is a question of all facts and circumstances based on the local market, but the church and minister have often already agreed on a figure and can provide documentary evidence.

The exclusion under IRC § 107 only applies if the employing church designates the amount of the parsonage allowance in advance of the tax year. The designation may appear in the minister's employment contract, the church minutes, the church budget, or any other document indicating official action. Treas. Reg. § 1.107-1(b).

An additional requirement for purposes of IRC § 107 is that the fair rental value of the parsonage or parsonage allowance is not more than reasonable pay for the ministerial services performed.

The amount of the parsonage allowance excludible from gross income is the LEAST of:

- The amount actually used to provide a home,

- The amount officially designated as a housing allowance, or
- The fair rental value (FRV) of the home, including furnishings and appurtenances such as a garage plus the cost of utilities. IRC § 107(2).

The following examples illustrate the application of these rules. For simplification, assume that mortgage payments include property taxes and insurance.

Example 1

A is an ordained minister. She receives an annual salary of $36,000 and use of a parsonage which has a FRV of $800 a month, including utilities. She has an accountable plan for other business expenses such as travel. A's gross income for arriving at taxable income for Federal income tax purposes is $36,000, but for self-employment tax purposes it is $45,600 ($36,000 salary + $9,600 FRV of parsonage).

Example 2

B, an ordained minister, is vice president of academic affairs at Holy Bible Seminary. His compensation package includes a salary of $80,000 per year and a $30,000 housing allowance. His housing costs for the year included mortgage payments of $15,000, utilities of $3,000, and $3,600 for home maintenance and new furniture. The fair rental value of the home, as furnished, is $18,000 per year.

The three amounts for comparison are:

- Actual expenses of $21,600 ($15,000 mortgage payments + $3,000 utilities + $3,600 other costs)
- Designated housing allowance of $30,000
- FRV plus utilities of $21,000 ($18,000 + $3,000 utilities)

B may exclude $21,000 from gross income but must include in income the other $9,000 of the housing allowance. The entire $30,000 will be considered in arriving at net self-employment income.

Example 3

C is an ordained minister and has been in his church's employ for the last 20 years. His salary is $40,000 and his designated parsonage allowance is $15,000. C's mortgage was paid off last year. During the tax year he spent $2,000 on utilities, and $3,000 on real estate taxes and insurance. The FRV of his home, as furnished, is $750 a month.

The three amounts for comparison are:

- Actual housing costs of $5,000 ($2,000 utilities + $3,000 taxes and insurance)
- Designated housing allowance of $15,000
- FRV + utilities of $11,000 ($9,000 FRV + $2,000 utilities)

C may only exclude his actual expenses of $5,000 for Federal income tax purposes. He may not exclude the FRV of his home even though he has paid for it in previous years. *Swaggart v. Commissioner*, T.C. Memo. 1984-409. $15,000 will be included in the computation of net self-employment income.

Example 4

Assume the same facts as in Example 3, except that C takes out a home equity loan and uses the proceeds to pay for his daughter's college tuition. The payments are $300 per month. Even though he has a loan secured by his home, the money was not used to "provide a home" and can't be used to compute the excludible portion of the parsonage allowance. The results are the same as for Example 3. The interest on the home equity loan may be deducted as an itemized deduction subject to the limitations, if any, of IRC § 163.

Example 5

D is an ordained minister who received $40,000 in salary plus a designated housing allowance of $12,000. He spent $12,000 on mortgage payments, $2,400 on utilities, and $2,000 on new furniture. The FRV of his home as furnished is $16,000. D's exclusion is limited to $12,000 even though his actual cost ($16,400) and FRV and utilities ($18,400) are more. He may not deduct his housing costs in excess of the designated allowance.

Example 6

E's designated housing allowance is $20,000. She and her husband live in one half of a duplex which they own. The other half is rented. Mortgage payments for the duplex are $1,500 per month. E's utilities run $1,800 per year, and her tenant pays his own from a separate meter. During the year E replaced carpeting throughout the structure at a cost of $6,500 and did minor repairs of $500. E must allocate her mortgage costs, carpeting, and repairs between her own unit and the rental unit in determining the amount of the excludible parsonage allowance. Amounts allocable to the rented portion for mortgage interest, taxes, etc., would be reported on Schedule E as usual. Her actual costs to provide a home were $14,300 ($9,000 mortgage payments, $1,800 utilities, and $3,500 for half the carpeting and repairs). The FRV for her unit is the same as the rent she charges for the other half, which is $750 a month, and she estimates that her furnishings add another $150 per month to the FRV. Her FRV plus utilities is $12,600 ($10,800 FRV + $1,800 utilities). E may exclude $12,600 for Federal income tax purposes.

Pursuant to IRC § 265(a)(6) and Rev. Rul. 87-32, 1987-1 C.B. 131 even though a minister's home mortgage interest and real estate taxes have been paid with money excluded from income as a housing allowance, he or she may still claim itemized deductions for these items. The sale of the residence is treated the same as that of other taxpayers, even though it may have been completely purchased with funds excluded under IRC § 107. Because expenses attributable to earned income which is exempt from tax are not ordinarily deductible, a minister's business expenses related to his or her earnings must be allocated and become partially nondeductible pursuant to IRC § 265 This is discussed in detail in the section on Business Expenses.

Exhibit 1 provides a worksheet for the computation of the amount that is excludible as a parsonage allowance

Retired Ministers

A retired minister may receive part of his or her pension benefits as a designated parsonage allowance based on past services. Trustees of a minister's retirement plan may designate a portion of each pension distribution as a parsonage allowance excludible under IRC § 107. (Rev. Rul. 63-156, 1963-2 C.B. 79, and Rev. Rul. 75-22, 1975-1, C.B. 49) The "least of" rules should be applied to determine the amount excludible from gross income.

The retired minister may exclude from his/her net earnings from self-employment the rental value of the parsonage or the parsonage allowance received after retirement. The entire amount of parsonage allowance received is excludible from net earnings from self employment, even if a portion of it is not excludible for income tax purposes. In addition, the retired minister may exclude from net earnings from self-employment any retirement benefits received from a church plan. Rev. Rul. 58-359, 1958-2 C.B. 422.

Members of Religious Orders and Vow of Poverty
If you are a member of an exempt religious order who has taken a vow of poverty, you are exempt from income tax and self

employment tax on your earnings for qualified services you perform as an "agent" of your church or its agencies. The religious order must be an organization described in IRC § 170(c)(2). Rev. Rul. 76-323, 1976-2 C.B. 18, stated "Amounts received by members of an exempt religious order, not acting as agents of the order, for work performed outside the religious community and paid over, in full or part, to the order at its direction, are includible in the gross incomes of the members and are wages subject to the FICA and income tax withholding. However, the individual members are entitled to charitable contribution deductions under IRC § 170 for amounts donated to the order." The ruling stated in reference to performance as an "agent" that "ordinarily a member is performing services as the agent of the religious order only if the order is engaged in the performance of the services as a principal. Ordinarily an order is not engaged in the performance of services as a principal where the legal relationship of employer and employee exists between the member and the third party with respect to the performance of such services."

The United States Court of Appeals for the Federal Circuit in *Reverend Gerald P Fogarty, S.J. v the United States*, 780 F.2d 1005, 1012 (Fed. Cir. 1986), provided a flexible facts and circumstance test for determining if the member is acting as an agent for the order or in their individual capacity. The Court stated the relevant facts to consider are:

"The presence of unique facts in each case will inevitably lead the court to place more emphasis on one or more factors and less on others. The relationship between the order and the member gives rise to a number of factors. Relevant considerations there will include the degree of control exercised by the order over the member as well as the ownership rights between member and order, *Kelley v. Commissioner*, 62 T.C. 131 (1974), the purposes or mission of the order, and the type of work performed by the member vis-a-vis those purposes or mission, ...

Other factors will include the dealings between the member and the third-party employer (circumstances surrounding job inquiries and interviews, and control or supervision exercised by the employer), and dealings between the employer and order." Id. The outcome of the case was that the Appeals Court ruled that the income earned by Reverend Fogarty, a member of the Society of Jesus religious order, as a professor at the University of Virginia, Department of Religious Studies, was taxable to him. He was not acting as an agent of the order.

The U.S. Court of Appeals for the Seventh Circuit, in *Francince Schuster v. Commissioner*, 800 F.2d 672, 678-79 (7th Cir. 1986), ruled the earned income of a nun, a member of a religious order who worked as a nurse in a clinic in the employment of the National Health Services Corps, was taxable to her as an individual and not as an agent of the order. The Court applied the six factors above to the facts of the case in making its determination.

Likewise the U.S. States Court of Appeals for the Federal Circuit in *Jerome G. Kircher, O.F.M. and Valens Waldschmidt, O.F.M. v. The United States*, 872 F.2d 1014, 1018-20 (Fed. Cir. 1989), applied the six factors above to the facts of the case in making its determination that the taxpayers, priests who were members of a religious order who worked as chaplains in a leper hospital and a mental hospital, earned income was taxable to them and not as an agent for the order.

In Rev. Rul. 77-290, 1977-2 C.B. 26, the earned income of an attorney who was a member of a religious order who has taken a vow of poverty, was taxable to him and not the order even though the income was directly deposited in the order's bank account. It also determined that a secretary, who was also a member of the same order, who worked on the direction of the order at the business office of the church that supervises the order, was acting as an agent for the order and the earned income was not taxable to the secretary.

In Rev. Rul. 79-132, 1979-1 C.B. 62, the earned income a military chaplain who was a member of a religious order who has taken a vow of poverty, was taxable to him and not the order even though he turned over the remuneration to the order.

Research and Source for this answer: IRS Minister Audit Technique Guide Publication date - April 2009.

CHAPTER 6 - What should I do if our church or Corporation Sole is ever presented with a certified letter notice from the IRS for either a formal IRS audit, intent to levy or a formal church Inquiry?

Answer: First, if your church ever receives a letter from the IRS, DO NOT FREAK OUT! You are both a child of the most high God and according to Romans 8:37, which states, *"in all these things we are **more than conquerors** through him who loved us."*! Never be fearful of the Government, and remember that anytime you receive a letter from the IRS, it is considered an offer according to contract law. Each time they send you a letter they are attempting to establish or invoke jurisdiction over either you personally, your church or your subsequent Corporation Sole. In contract law, an acceptance may be conditional, express, or implied.

Let me explain each in detail:

Conditional Acceptance A conditional acceptance, sometimes called a qualified acceptance, occurs when a person to whom an offer has been made tells the party (which in this case, we'll pretend it is the IRS) that he or she is willing to agree to the offer provided that some changes are made in its terms or that some condition or event occurs. This type of acceptance operates as a counteroffer. A counteroffer must be accepted by the original party before a contract can be established between the parties.

Express Acceptance An express acceptance occurs when a person clearly and explicitly agrees to an offer or agrees to pay a draft that is presented for payment.

Implied Acceptance An implied acceptance is one that is not directly stated but is demonstrated by any acts indicating a person's assent to the proposed bargain. An implied acceptance occurs when a shopper selects an item in a supermarket and pays the cashier for it. The shopper's conduct indicates that he or she has agreed to the supermarket owner's offer to sell the item for the price stated on it. In addition, if you do nothing and remain silent regarding the IRS's offer, then your silence is considered your acquiescence (meaning, you have consented under silence). The legal basis for this is found in the following cases: *Connally v. General Construction Co.*, 269 U.S. 385, 391. Notification of legal responsibility is "the first essential of due process of law." Also, see: *U.S. v. Tweel*, 550 F. 2d. 297. "Silence can only be equated with fraud where there is a legal or moral duty to speak or where an inquiry left unanswered would be intentionally misleading."

We recommend that if the IRS sends your church an official notice, that it is replied to immediately with a Conditional Acceptance letter.

The type of language contained in this conditional acceptance letter needs to be very strong. Here is an example of a typical conditional acceptance letter we would send the IRS:

--------BEGINNING OF CONDITIONAL ACCEPTANCE LETTER------

CHURCH NAME HERE
PO Box 1111
any town, any state [55555]

Month day, year

CERTIFIED MAIL return receipt
#_____

To: Name of IRS employee,
    Employee Identification Number: 11111
    C/o INTERNAL REVENUE SERVICE

P.O. Box 1,
ANYTOWN, ANYSTATE 55555-5566

Re: XXX-XX-1111

LAWFUL NOTIFICATION – CONDITIONAL ACCEPTANCE NOTICE

This letter is lawful notification to you, pursuant to The Bill of Rights of the National Constitution, in particular, the First, Fourth, Fifth, Sixth and Ninth Amendments, and the Constitution of (name of state here), in particular, Article 1, Declaration of Rights, pursuant to your oath, and requires your written response to me specific to the subject matter. In good faith, our Church, (CHURCH NAME HERE), conditionally accepts your request for more information upon bona fide proof of claim supported by truth, fact and evidence and complete answers to the following good faith and material questions be timely answered. Your failure to respond, within 21 days, as stipulated, and rebut, with particularity, everything in this letter with which you disagree is your lawful, legal and binding agreement with and admission to the fact that everything in this letter is true, correct, legal, lawful and binding upon you, in any court, anywhere in America, without your protest or objection or that of those who represent you and that this matter is settled in its entirety and that our Church, (CHURCH NAME HERE), is in fact a bona fide Church that is mandatorily exempted from taxation and mandatorily exempted from filing annual information returns pursuant to both 26 U.S.C § 508(c)(1)(a) and 26 U.S.C § 6033(3)(a)(1-3). Your silence is your acquiescence. See: *Connally v. General Construction Co.*, 269 U.S. 385, 391. Notification of legal responsibility is "the first essential of due process of law." Also, see: *U.S. v. Tweel*, 550 F. 2d. 297. "Silence can only be equated with fraud where there is a legal or moral duty to speak or where an inquiry left unanswered would be intentionally misleading."

Please take lawful notice that in order to effect this BONA FIDE PROOF, THE UNITED STATES DEPARTMENT OF THE TREASURY and The INTERNAL REVENUE SERVICE via a legally authorized representative are lawfully required and hereby demanded to respond point by point, in Truth, Fact and Evidence via oath of affirmation under penalty of perjury to each and every single particular item set forth in this correspondence before our Authorized Representative can make an offer to settle the INTERNAL REVENUE SERVICE'S alleged claim or request for more information in this matter.

Please Provide Specific Answers Supported by a valid Oath of Affirmation for EACH of the Following Particular Numbered Conditions:

CONDITION #1: Pursuant to United States Supreme Court Ruling, **Sherar v. Cullen, 481 F.945**, that, *"For a crime to exist, there must be an injured party (Corpus Delicti), There can be no sanction or penalty imposed on one because of this Constitutional right."* Therefor, we demand material evidence supported by an oath of affirmation, under penalty of perjury, where the United States, Department of the Treasury and or The Internal Revenue Service, is in fact an injured or damaged party related to our Church, (CHURCH NAME HERE).

CONDITION #2: In order for us to lawfully ascertain that you are in fact, an employee of the Internal Revenue Service, you are required to have an oath of office on file for public scrutiny, specifically referenced in U.S.C Title 5 Chapter 33 Subsection 3331, and bonds to guarantee your faithful performance of your duties, pursuant to your oath, as the law requires. We respectfully demand that you send us a certified copy of your timely filed oath of office and copies of all bonds you are required to obtain according to law. If you fail to provide these, then you admit that you have no oath of office, no bonds as required by law and no malpractice insurance.

CONDITION #3: Being that you're lawfully required to have sworn an oath to uphold and support the Constitution of the United States of America, and pursuant to your oath, you are required to abide by that oath in the performance of your official duties. Therefor, Pursuant to the 5th Amendment to the Constitution, the supreme law of the land, which specifically states, *"nor shall be compelled in any criminal case to be a witness against himself, nor be deprived of life, liberty, or property, without due process of law; nor shall private property be taken for public use, without just compensation."* We demand you provide us via a signed sworn affidavit under penalty of perjury with evidence of what constitutionally valid American Law, if any, has changed or made void, the above-cited constitutionally valid 5th Amendment.

CONDITION #4: A copy of a signed IRS Form 1023, that shows with truth, fact and evidence, that our Church, (CHURCH NAME HERE) in fact, has either applied for, sought or accepted the Internal Revenue Service's official recognition of our mandatory tax exempt status as provided to us by law pursuant to 26 U.S.C § 508(c)(1)(a).

CONDITION #5: We demand material evidence supported by an oath of affirmation, under penalty of perjury, where our Church, (CHURCH NAME HERE), has in fact rescinded our privileged right to mandatory tax exemption pursuant to 26 U.S.C § 508(c)(1)(a).

CONDITION #6: We demand material evidence supported by an oath of affirmation, under penalty of perjury where our Church, (CHURCH NAME HERE), has in fact rescinded our privileged right to mandatory be exempted from filing annual information returns to the Internal Revenue Service pursuant to 26 U.S.C § 6033(3)(a)(1-3).

Again, your failure to respond, within 21 days, as stipulated, and rebut, with particularity, everything in this letter with which you disagree is your lawful, legal and binding agreement with and admission to the fact that everything in this letter is true, correct, legal, lawful and binding upon you, in any court, anywhere in America, without your protest or objection or that of those who represent you and that this matter is settled in its entirety and that our Church, (CHURCH NAME HERE), is in fact a bona fide Church that is mandatorily exempted from taxation and mandatorily exempted from filing annual information returns pursuant to both 26 U.S.C § 508(c)(1)(a) and 26 U.S.C § 6033(3)(a)(1-3). Your silence is your acquiescence.

Sincerely,

Full Legal Name Here, American Citizen, as acting overseer for, CHURCH NAME HERE, a 26 U.S.C § 508(c)(1)(a) Church.
All Rights Reserved, without Prejudice.

--------END OF LETTER-------------

These type of letters need to be sent via certified delivery, signature return receipt via the United States Postal Service and via notary certificate immediately upon receiving an IRS notice. Make sure to keep the original, 'wet inked' copy of the notary certificate and include a copy of the notary certificate with the conditional acceptance letter your are sending to the IRS.

Here is an example of a notary certificate (which will need to be signed by a notary prior to sending):

--------BEGINNING OF NOTARY CERTIFICATE----------

NOTARY'S CERTIFICATE OF SERVICES

The services in this matter are done on behalf of FULL LEGAL NAME HERE, American Citizen.

It is hereby certified that on this ___ day of _____, 2012, I, FULL LEGAL NAME HERE, authorize the undersigned Notary Public to Mail these Documents to:

NAME OF RECIPIENT
STREET ADDRESS
CITY, STATE-ZIP CODE
TELEPHONE

Hereinafter, "Recipient", the documents and sundry papers which include the following:

1. NAME OF RECIPIENT – **LAWFUL NOTIFICATION – CONDITIONAL ACCEPTANCE NOTICE LETTER**
2. Copy of Notary Certificate

By certified mail number, _____Notary Public, by placing the same in postpaid envelope, properly addressed to Recipient at the said address and depositing the same at an official depository under the exclusive face and custody of the U.S. Postal Service within the State of _____

Notary Public Signature as Witness to Documents:_____

I, FULL LEGAL NAME HERE, certify under penalties of perjury that these Documents have been witnessed on this ___ day of _____, 2012, and all the Documents being sent out are true and correct to the best of my knowledge.

Signature_____Date:_____
FULL LEGAL NAME HERE

State of_____
County of _____

Subscribed and sworn to (or affirmed) before me on this ____ day of _____, 2012 by FULL LEGAL NAME HERE, proved to me on the basis of satisfactory evidence to be the person(s) who appeared before me.

_____ (Seal)
Notary Public

--------END OF NOTARY CERTIFICATE----------

IMPORTANT NOTE: *DO NOT ACCEPT their common 45 day deferral letter "offer" they may send in response, where they say they need more time. Any frivolous filing letter is also an "offer". They are trying to make you concede the time line and default. If this happens, quickly send our NOTICE OF DEFAULT – INSUFFICIENT RESPONSE letter (listed below) declining to accept their offer to extend the time to investigate. You have given the required time as required by law. When you send the follow-up, insufficient response/notice of default letter, also make sure that you send that via certified delivery, signature return receipt via the United States Postal Service and via notary certificate as well.*

Here is the NOTICE OF DEFAULT - INSUFFICIENT RESPONSE letter bellow:

---BEGINNING OF NOTICE OF DEFAULT - INSUFFICIENT RESPONSE ---

CHURCH NAME HERE
PO Box 1111
any town, any state [55555]

Month day, year

CERTIFIED MAIL return receipt
#_____

To: Name of IRS employee,
   Employee Identification Number: 11111
   C/o INTERNAL REVENUE SERVICE

   P.O. Box 1,
   ANYTOWN, ANYSTATE 55555-5566

Re: XXX-XX-1111 – NOTICE OF DEFAULT - INSUFFICIENT RESPONSE

NOTICE OF DEFAULT

For due process purposes, this NOTICE OF DEFAULT - INSUFFICIENT RESPONSE letter is lawful notification to you (NAME OF IRS EMPLOYEE WITH EMPLOYEE NUMBER), that your reply received on (DATE HERE) and offer to request to our Church, (CHURCH NAME HERE) for extended time to complete your investigation is hereby declined. You have been given the required time as required by law via our previous **LAWFUL NOTIFICATION – CONDITIONAL ACCEPTANCE NOTICE** letter sent to you via notary certificate, USPS certified delivery return receipt and received by you on (DATE OF THEM RECEIVING THE ORIGINAL LETTER HERE). Therefor, your reply is considered an insufficient response and a default on your part. Pursuant to the conditions set forth in our **LAWFUL NOTIFICATION – CONDITIONAL ACCEPTANCE NOTICE** and received by you on (DATE OF THEM RECEIVING THE ORIGINAL LETTER HERE), your failure to respond, within 21 days, as stipulated, and rebut, with particularity, everything in that letter with which you disagreed is your lawful, legal and binding agreement with and admission to the fact that everything in that letter was true, correct, legal, lawful and binding upon you, in any court, anywhere in America, without your protest or objection or that of those who represent you and that this matter has been settled in its entirety and that our Church, (CHURCH NAME HERE), is in fact a bona fide Church that is mandatorily exempted from taxation and mandatorily exempted from filing annual information returns pursuant to both 26 U.S.C § 508(c)(1)(a) and 26 U.S.C § 6033(3)(a)(1-3).

Please take lawful notice that in order for you to have met the conditions for our Church, (CHURCH NAME HERE) to fully accept your request for more information, that the bona fide proof the UNITED STATES DEPARTMENT OF THE TREASURY, (NAME OF IRS EMPLOYEE WITH EMPLOYEE NUMBER) and The INTERNAL REVENUE SERVICE via a legally authorized representative was lawfully required and thereby demanded to respond within 21 days as stipulated, point by point, in Truth, Fact and Evidence to each and every single particular item set forth in that **LAWFUL NOTIFICATION – CONDITIONAL ACCEPTANCE NOTICE**.

As of (TODAYS DATE), neither (NAME OF IRS AGENT – EMPLOYEE ID NUMBER) as an agent working for the INTERNAL REVENUE SERVICE nor the UNITED STATES DEPARTMENT OF THE TREASURY have given us any truth, fact or evidence supported by a valid oath of affirmation under penalty of perjury related to each particular condition(s) which were submitted and received by you on (DATE OF THEM RECEIVING THE ORIGINAL LETTER HERE). Those particular conditions were as follows:

> **CONDITION #1:** Pursuant to United States Supreme Court Ruling, **Sherar v. Cullen, 481 F.945**, that, *"For a crime to exist, there must be an injured party (Corpus Delicti), There can be no sanction or penalty imposed on one because of this Constitutional right."* Therefor, we demand material evidence supported by an oath of affirmation, under penalty of perjury, where the United States, Department of the Treasury and or The Internal Revenue Service, is in fact an injured or

damaged party related to our Church, (CHURCH NAME HERE).

CONDITION #2: In order for us to lawfully ascertain that you are in fact, an employee of the Internal Revenue Service, you are required to have an oath of office on file for public scrutiny, specifically referenced in U.S.C Title 5 Chapter 33 Subsection 3331, and bonds to guarantee your faithful performance of your duties, pursuant to your oath, as the law requires. We respectfully demand that you send us a certified copy of your timely filed oath of office and copies of all bonds you are required to obtain according to law. If you fail to provide these, then you admit that you have no oath of office, no bonds as required by law and no malpractice insurance.

CONDITION #3: Being that your lawfully required to have sworn an oath to uphold and support the Constitution of the United States of America, and pursuant to your oath, you are required to abide by that oath in the performance of your official duties. Therefor, Pursuant to the 5th Amendment to the Constitution, the supreme law of the land, which specifically states, *"nor shall be compelled in any criminal case to be a witness against himself, nor be deprived of life, liberty, or property, without due process of law; nor shall private property be taken for public use, without just compensation."* We demand you provide us via a signed sworn affidavit under penalty of perjury with evidence of what constitutionally valid American Law, if any, has changed or made void, the above-cited constitutionally valid 5th Amendment.

CONDITION #4: A copy of a signed IRS Form 1023, that shows with truth, fact and evidence, that our Church, (CHURCH NAME HERE) in fact, has either applied for, sought or accepted the Internal Revenue Service's official recognition of our mandatory tax exempt status as provided to us by law pursuant to 26 U.S.C § 508(c)(1)(a).

CONDITION #5: We demand material evidence supported by an oath of affirmation, under penalty of perjury, where our Church, (CHURCH NAME HERE), has in fact rescinded our privileged right to mandatory tax exemption pursuant to 26 U.S.C § 508(c)(1)(a).

CONDITION #6: We demand material evidence supported by an oath of affirmation, under penalty of perjury where our Church, (CHURCH NAME HERE), has in fact rescinded our privileged right to mandatory be exempted from filing annual information returns to the Internal Revenue Service pursuant to 26 U.S.C § 6033(3)(a)(1-3).

Therefor, Pursuant to CONDITION #1, as of (TODAYS DATE), neither (NAME OF IRS AGENT – EMPLOYEE ID NUMBER) as an agent working for the INTERNAL REVENUE SERVICE nor the UNITED STATES DEPARTMENT OF THE TREASURY have given us any truth, fact or evidence supported by a valid oath of affirmation under penalty of perjury that either the INTERNAL REVENUE SERVICE nor the UNITED STATES DEPARMENT OF THE TREASURY is in fact either a injured or damaged party related to our Church, (CHURCH NAME HERE) as required by law and pursuant to United States Supreme Court ruling **Sherar v. Cullen, 481 F.945**, which states, *"For a crime to exist, there must be an injured party (Corpus Delicti), There can be no sanction or penalty imposed on one because of this Constitutional right."*

And, Pursuant to CONDITION #2, as of (TODAYS DATE), that (NAME OF IRS AGENT – EMPLOYEE ID NUMBER) as an agent working for the INTERNAL REVENUE SERVICE has NOT given us their certified copy of their timely filed oath of office and copies of all bonds they are required to obtain according to U.S.C Title 5 Chapter 33 Subsection 3331. Because (NAME OF IRS AGENT – EMPLOYEE ID NUMBER) has failed to provide these, they have in fact admitted that they have no oath of office, no bonds as required by law and no malpractice insurance.

And, Pursuant to CONDITION #3, as of (TODAYS DATE), neither (NAME OF IRS AGENT – EMPLOYEE ID NUMBER) as an agent working for the INTERNAL REVENUE SERVICE nor the UNITED STATES DEPARTMENT OF THE TREASURY have given us any truth, fact or evidence supported by a valid oath of affirmation under penalty of perjury that there is in fact a constitutionally valid American Law, if any, that has changed or made void, the constitutionally valid 5th Amendment which states, *""nor shall be compelled in any criminal case to be a witness against himself, nor be deprived of life, liberty, or property, without due process of law; nor shall private property be taken for public use, without just compensation."*

And, Pursuant to CONDITION #4, as of (TODAYS DATE), neither (NAME OF IRS AGENT – EMPLOYEE ID NUMBER) as an agent working for the INTERNAL REVENUE SERVICE nor the UNITED STATES DEPARTMENT OF THE TREASURY have given us any truth, fact or evidence supported by a valid oath of affirmation under penalty of perjury that our Church, (CHURCH NAME HERE) has in fact either applied for, sought or accepted the Internal Revenue Service's official recognition of our mandatory tax exempt status as provided to us by law pursuant to 26 U.S.C § 508(c)(1)(a) nor given us a signed IRS Form 1023 showing where we have contractually accepted or sought the Internal Revenue Service's Conditions for our Mandatory Tax Exemption as provided by 26 U.S.C § 508(c)(1)(a).

And, Pursuant to CONDITION #5, as of (TODAYS DATE), neither (NAME OF IRS AGENT – EMPLOYEE ID NUMBER) as an agent working for the INTERNAL REVENUE SERVICE nor the UNITED STATES DEPARTMENT OF THE TREASURY have given us any truth, fact or evidence supported by a valid oath of affirmation under penalty of perjury that our Church, (CHURCH NAME HERE) has in fact rescinded our privileged right to mandatory tax exemption pursuant to 26 U.S.C § 508(c)(1)(a).

And, Pursuant to CONDITION #6, as of (TODAYS DATE), neither (NAME OF IRS AGENT – EMPLOYEE ID NUMBER) as an agent working for the INTERNAL REVENUE SERVICE nor the UNITED STATES DEPARTMENT OF THE TREASURY have given us any truth, fact or evidence supported by a valid oath of affirmation under penalty of perjury that our Church, (CHURCH NAME HERE) has in fact rescinded our privileged right to mandatorily be exempted from filing annual information returns to the Internal Revenue Service pursuant to 26 U.S.C § 6033(3)(a)(1-3).

Due to your failure to respond, within the 21 days from the date of (DATE OF THEM RECEIVING THE ORIGINAL LETTER HERE), where we have signature proof of your receipt of our **LAWFUL NOTIFICATION – CONDITIONAL ACCEPTANCE NOTICE** as stipulated, and failure to rebut, with particularity, everything contained in our previous **LAWFUL NOTIFICATION – CONDITIONAL ACCEPTANCE NOTICE** with which you could have disagreed, is your lawful, legal and binding agreement with and admission to the fact that everything in our **LAWFUL NOTIFICATION – CONDITIONAL ACCEPTANCE NOTICE** letter was true, correct, legal, lawful and binding upon you, in any court, anywhere in America, without any protest or objection or that of those who represent you and that this matter is finally settled in its entirety and that our Church, (CHURCH NAME HERE), is in fact a bona fide Church that is mandatorily exempted from taxation and mandatorily exempted from filing annual information returns pursuant to both 26 U.S.C § 508(c)(1)(a) and 26 U.S.C § 6033(3)(a)(1-3).

Thank you for bringing final resolution to this very important matter.

Sincerely,

Full Legal Name Here, American Citizen, as acting overseer for, CHURCH NAME HERE, a 26 U.S.C § 508(c)(1)(a) Church.
All Rights Reserved, without Prejudice.

---END OF NOTICE OF DEFAULT - INSUFFICIENT RESPONSE LETTER---

And here is the follow up notary certificate you should use:

--------BEGINNING OF 2nd NOTARY CERTIFICATE----------

NOTARY'S CERTIFICATE OF SERVICES

The services in this matter are done on behalf of FULL LEGAL NAME HERE, American Citizen.

It is hereby certified that on this ___ day of _____, 2012, I, FULL LEGAL NAME HERE, authorize the undersigned Notary Public to Mail these Documents to:

NAME OF RECIPIENT
STREET ADDRESS
CITY, STATE-ZIP CODE
TELEPHONE

Hereinafter, "Recipient", the documents and sundry papers which include the following:

1. NAME OF RECIPIENT – NOTICE OF DEFAULT - INSUFFICIENT RESPONSE LETTER
2. Copy of Notary Certificate

By certified mail number,_____
Notary Public, by placing the same in postpaid envelope, properly addressed to Recipient at the said address and depositing the same at an official depository under the exclusive face and custody of the U.S. Postal Service within the State of _____

Notary Public Signature as Witness to Documents:_____

I, FULL LEGAL NAME HERE, certify under penalties of perjury that these Documents have been witnessed on this ____ day of _____, 2012, and all the Documents being sent out are true and correct to the best of my knowledge.

Signature_____Date:_____
FULL LEGAL NAME HERE

State of_____
County of _____

Subscribed and sworn to (or affirmed) before me on this ____ day of _____, 2012 by FULL LEGAL NAME HERE, proved to me on the basis of satisfactory evidence to be the person(s) who appeared before me.

_____ (Seal)
Notary Public

--------END OF 2nd NOTARY CERTIFICATE----------

ORDAINING OTHERS

CHAPTER 7 – As an Overseer or Bishop, I would like to ordain ministers underneath our covering of ministry, am I able to do this with a Corporation Sole?

<u>YES!</u> In this section we have provided a custom Church Establishment Affidavit that simultaneously creates BOTH an association Church as well as ordains a pastor you wish to lead this new association Church. We have also provided you with an additional second amendment to this affidavit that allows for this association Church to properly assign the positions of both successor and secretary to the new association Church's subsequent Corporation Sole. It's important to point out that this association Church is MANDATORILY exempted from taxation as well as being required to file annual information returns to the Internal Revenue Service. This is pursuant to both 26 U.S.C § 508(c)(1)(a) and 26 U.S.C § 6033(3)(A)(1-3) which state the following:

26 U.S.C § 508(c)(1)(a), states,

> (a) **New organizations must notify Secretary that they are applying for recognition of section 501(c)(3) status**
> Except as provided in subsection (c), an organization organized after October 9, 1969, **shall not** be treated as an organization described in section 501(c)(3)

Specifically section (c)(1)(a), which reads,

> (c) **Exceptions**
> (1) **Mandatory exceptions**
> Subsections (a) and (b) shall not apply to—
> (A) churches, their integrated auxiliaries, and conventions or **<u>associations of churches</u>**

And then 26 U.S.C § 6033(3)(A)(1-3) which covers,

> (3) **Exceptions from filing**
> (A) **<u>Mandatory exceptions</u>**

134

Paragraph (1) shall not apply to—
(i) *churches, their integrated auxiliaries, and conventions or* **_associations of churches_**,
(ii) any organization (other than a private foundation, as defined in section 509 (a)) described in subparagraph (C), the gross receipts of which in each taxable year are normally not more than $5,000, or
(iii) the exclusively religious activities of any religious order.

With this affidavit, your ministry will be able to establish as many association Churches as it wishes and ordain as many pastors as the Lord allows you to!

In addition, the Association Church will also be able to organize their financial structure with a Corporation Sole as well. Instead of being listed as either a Bishop or Overseer, their corporation sole will reflect the name of their association church as well as their position as a Pastor.

Hypothetical Example:

- Our Church is called, The Empowerment Center *(which is entirely under the jurisdiction of 26 U.S.C § 508(c)(1)(a) NOT 501c3).*
- Our Primary Church's Corporation Sole is called, "The Empowerment Center Overseer and Successors, a Corporation Sole. *(Which is entirely under the jurisdiction of 26 U.S.C § 501(c)(3)).*

- Our Association Church is called, "Redemption Church" which has a newly ordained Pastor using our affidavit below. *(This association Church is entirely under the jurisdiction of 26 U.S.C § 508(c)(1)(a) NOT 501c3).*
- Our Association Church's Corporation Sole is called, "Redemption Church Pastor and Successors, a Corporation Sole". *(Which is entirely under the jurisdiction of 26 U.S.C § 501(c)(3)).*

IMPORTANT: Ordinations and the creation of Association Church's are VERY important parts to growing any ministry. Therefor, it is important to note whenever your ordaining a Pastor or creating a legal entity such an Association Church, that the main Church is legally responsible for all actions taken on the behalf of the Association Church or ministry. For instance, if your Church decides to ordain a Pastor only to later find out the man/woman is either a pedophile, adulterer, con-artist or criminal and they commit any act which causes someone to be harmed in anyway (regardless if its financial, emotional, sexual or otherwise) then as the parent Church, you are responsible for all actions your Association Church participated in. So, make sure you have prayed and sought counsel from your Churches elders before ordaining anyone. DO NOT lightly ordain just anyone. Make sure you use 1st Timothy chapter 3 as a benchmark for ANYONE seeking a position of leadership in the Lords Church.

Here are the Affidavits:

*Note: Simply replace the following words:

REPLACE: (Church Name Here) – with the name of the Parent Church.
REPLACE: (Pastors Name Here) – with name of current Church Overseer.
REPLACE: (Pastors Spouse) – with name of either the (Pastors Spouse) or whoever is the acting Successor to your Churches Corporation Sole.
REPLACE: New Church Name Here – with the name of the new Association Church name.
REPLACE: Ordained (Pastors Name Here) – with the full legal name of the person you are ordaining to become the Pastor of the new Association Church.
REPLACE: (Successor Person) – with the full legal name of the person assigned to be the Association Church's Corporation Sole Successor.

REPLACE: (Secretary Person) – with the full legal name of the person assigned to be the Association Church's Corporation Sole Secretary.

----BEGIN ASSOCIATION CHURCH AND ORDINATION AFFIDAVIT-----

INTEGRATED AUXILIARIES AND CONVENTIONS OR ASSOCIATIONS OF CHURCHES AND ORDINATION OF MINISTRY LEADERSHIP UNDER THE AUTHORITY OF CHURCH NAME HERE AND (PASTORS NAME HERE) AS ACTING OVERSEER OF CHURCH NAME HERE

We, the undersigned declarant(s), on this _____ day of _____ in the Year of our Lord 20___, desiring to form Integrated Auxiliaries and Conventions or Associations or Churches and Ordaining certain ministry leaders in order to faithfully discharge the duties of maintaining such Church associations under the authority of Church Name Here and (Pastors Name Here) as acting Overseer of Church Name Here, hereby organize according to the following statute declaration(s) and article(s):

1. ASSOCIATION OF CHURCH NAME
   We, the declarant(s) (Pastors Name Here), (Pastors Spouse) and Ordained (Pastors Name Here), declare, affirm, manifest and recognize the formation of a new association Church under the governing authority of Church Name Here and (Pastors Name Here) as acting Overseer of Church Name Here. This new Association Church shall be called, New Church Name Here.

2. GOVERNING AUTHORITY
   Under the exclusive governing authority of Church Name Here and (Pastors Name Here) as acting Overseer of Church Name Here, that both (Pastors Name Here) and New Church Name Here, its members, attendees, associate pastor(s), elder(s), deacon(s), etc., shall submit to and be governed in accordance with God's Word, the Holy Bible, as well as the Church Name Here's Constitution, Articles of Faith, and other governing documents which may from time to time be prescribed by Church Name Here.

3. SCOPE OF POWERS

The Association Church, New Church Name Here acting through its Pastor(s), Elder(s), and any they may from time to time appoint, and shall be authorized to conduct Church activities and functions deemed necessary to the proper operation of the Church. Such activities shall include, but not be limited to, opening financial accounts such as bank accounts (whether checking, savings, etc.), as well as brokerage or other investment accounts, the purchase, lease or rental of church meeting facilities, as well as necessary office facilities, the purchase, lease or rental of church office equipment, musical instruments, sacerdotal accouterments, and any and all other forms of property, both real and personal, vehicles, equipment, supplies, implements or tools deemed necessary to the proper operation of the Church, the purchase of insurance, the remuneration or compensation of the Church's minister(s) such as its pastor(s) and other ministers, the distribution of tangible and intangible gifts or benevolent charities, as well as any other necessary and appropriate financial transactions, the association Church acting through its governing body, for the initiation, promotion, expansion and continuation of this ministry.

Current appointed and authorized Banking Checking or Savings Account Signatories for this association Church, New Church Name Here are as follows:

Authorized Banking Signatory #1: (Pastors Name Here), as acting pastor
Authorized Banking Signatory #2: (Pastors Spouse), as associate pastor

4. TAX EXEMPT STATUS
   Pursuant to 26 U.S.C § 508(c)(1)(a):

   (a) **New organizations must notify Secretary that they**

are applying for recognition of section 501(c)(3) status

Except as provided in subsection (c), an organization organized after October 9, 1969, **shall not** be treated as an organization described in section 501(c)(3)

Specifically section 508(c)(1)(a), which reads,

(c) **Exceptions**
(1) **Mandatory exceptions**
Subsections (a) and (b) shall not apply to—
(A) churches, their integrated auxiliaries, and conventions or associations of churches

AND in reference to the Internal Revenue Code Publication 557 and IRC Publication section 501(c)(3), our association Church, "New Church Name Here" formally declares that this is a MANDATORILY TAX EXEMPTED CHURCH and as such, **are ELIGIBLE TO RECEIVE TAX DEDUCTIBLE CONTRIBUTIONS** as Defined by both IRC Publication 557 and 501(c)(3), which states the following,

IRC PUBLICATION 557: *"Organizations Not Required To File Form 1023*

Some organizations **are not required** to file Form 1023. These include:

Churches, interchurch organizations of local units of a church, conventions or associations of churches, or integrated auxiliaries of a church, such as a men's or women's organization, religious school, mission society, or youth group.

These organizations are exempt automatically if they meet the requirements of section 501(c)(3)."

IRC Publication Section 501(c)(3) Definition of

"Churches":

Churches. Although a church, its integrated auxiliaries, or a convention or association of churches **is not required to file Form 1023 to be exempt from federal income tax or to receive tax deductible contributions**, the organization may find it advantageous to obtain recognition of exemption.

We, the declarant(s) (Pastors Name Here), (Pastors Spouse) and Ordained (Pastors Name Here), declare, "New Church Name Here" <u>DOES NOT</u> find it 'advantageous' to 'obtain recognition of exemption' from the Internal Revenue Service as we respectfully retain and declare our sovereign right to remain a **Tax Exempt Church** as prescribed and described above and because the First Amendment of The Constitution of The United States of America clearly states, "**Congress shall make no law respecting an establishment of religion**, or prohibiting the free exercise thereof; or abridging the freedom of speech, or of the press; or the right of the people peaceably to assemble, and to petition the government for a redress of grievances."

We DECLARE and AFFIRM that we, "The Church" are AUTOMATICALLY considered TAX EXEMPT from Federal Income Tax, Property Tax and that ALL Tithe and Offering contribution(s) shall be considered Tax Deductible pursuant to law.

5. DISTINCT LEGAL EXISTENCE

This affidavit serves to fulfill 28 USC § 1746 regarding sworn declarations under penalty of perjury. We, the declarant(s) (Pastors Name Here), (Pastors Spouse) and Ordained (Pastors Name Here), declare and affirm under the penalties of perjury the recognized and distinct lawful existence of New Church Name Here as a bona fide Association Church of Church Name Here.

6. RECOGNIZED CREED AND FORM OF WORSHIP

We, the declarant(s) (Pastors Name Here), (Pastors Spouse) and Ordained (Pastors Name Here), declare, affirm that New Church Name Here has a recognized creed and form of worship through our faith in Jesus Christ. We believe the Bible to be the inspired, infallible, authoritative Word of God. We believe in the deity of our Lord Jesus Christ, in His virgin birth, in His sinless life, in His miracles, in His vicarious and atoning death through His shed blood, in His bodily resurrection, in His ascension to the right hand of the Father, and in His personal return in power and glory.

7. FORMAL CODE OF DOCTRINE AND DISCIPLINE

We, the declarant(s) (Pastors Name Here), (Pastors Spouse) and Ordained (Pastors Name Here), declare, affirm and recognize four distinct doctrines:

1. Salvation Through Jesus Christ.
2. The Manifestation of the Divine Gifts of the Spirit (as Described in 1st Corinthians 12).
3. Upon being born again, our salvation is sealed with the baptism of the Holy Spirit.
4. The Second Coming of Jesus Christ.

We also believe and practice three ordinances:

1. Water Baptism by Immersion after repenting of one's sins and receiving Christ's gift of salvation.
2. Holy Communion (the Lord's Supper) as a symbolic remembrance of Christ's suffering and death for our salvation.
3. That we make every effort to do what leads to peace and mutual edification for ALL practicing members in the Body of Christ.

8. ASSOCIATION CHURCH – LITERATURE OF ITS OWN

We, the declarant(s) (Pastors Name Here), (Pastors Spouse) and Ordained (Pastors Name Here), declare and affirm that this Church Establishment Affidavit and its various statements of New Church Name Here's faith, doctrines and ordinances shall be publically known and will serve as literature of its own accord.

9. ESTABLISHED PLACE(S) OF WORSHIP, REGULAR CONGREGATION(S) AND REGULAR RELIGIOUS SERVICES

We, the declarant(s) (Pastors Name Here), (Pastors Spouse) and Ordained (Pastors Name Here), declare and affirm as a fellowship of believers, that New Church Name Here holds regular services for the empowerment and spiritual equipping for the benefit to the Body of Christ. We affirm and declare under penalties of perjury that the specific meeting places for these times of worship may vary to locations such as a leased or owned building(s) or house(s), public property(s), meeting hall(s), restaurant(s), coffee shop(s), radio communication(s), conference call(s), cell phone conversation(s), online webinar(s), forum(s) and all forms of digital communication(s), such as but not limited to website domain(s) that allow for the gathering of members of "New Church Name Here".

10. RELIGIOUS INSTRUCTION OF THE YOUNG

We, the declarant(s) (Pastors Name Here), (Pastors Spouse) and Ordained (Pastors Name Here), declare and affirm under the penalties of perjury the practice of instructing the young in the ways of the Lord.

11. PREPARATION FOR MINISTER(S)

We, the declarant(s) (Pastors Name Here), (Pastors Spouse) and Ordained (Pastors Name Here), declare and affirm under the penalties of perjury that if a member of New Church Name Here desires to become an ordained minister, that they must have their house in Godly order as described in 1st Timothy chapter Three. 1st Timothy chapter Three shall serve as a guide to being qualified for ordination here at New Church Name Here. Ordination shall be prescribed only by the discretion of authorized Church personal such as Ordained (Pastors Name Here) as acting Pastor and by the laying on of hands and with the anointing of oil by the New Church Here's elder(s).

12. MANDATORY EXEMPTION FROM FILING ANNUAL INFORMATION RETURNS TO THE INTERNAL REVENUE SERVICE

We, the declarant(s) (Pastors Name Here), (Pastors Spouse) and Ordained (Pastors Name Here), declare and affirm under the penalties of perjury that pursuant to 26 U.S.C § 6033(3)(A)(1-3), which states,

(3) **Exceptions from filing**
(A) **Mandatory exceptions**
Paragraph (1) shall not apply to—
(i) *churches, their integrated auxiliaries, and conventions or associations of churches*,
(ii) any organization (other than a private foundation, as defined in section 509 (a)) described in subparagraph (C), the gross receipts of which in each taxable year are normally not more than $5,000, or
(iii) *the exclusively religious activities of any religious order.*

That our Association Church, New Church Name Here and it's future subsequent Corporation Sole, New Church Name Here Pastor and Successors, a Corporation Sole are MANDATORILY exempted from filing annual information returns to the Internal Revenue Service.

13. ORGANIZATION OF ORDAINED MINISTER(S) AND ORDAINED MINISTER(S) SELECTED AFTER COMPLETING PRESCRIBED STUDIES

We, the declarant(s) (Pastors Name Here) as acting Overseer of Church Name Here and (Pastors Spouse) as a member of Church Name Here, declare and affirm under the penalties of perjury that Ordained (Pastors Name Here) has completed a competent amount of biblical studies and is hereby ordained as Pastor of New Church Name Here.

14. AUTHORIZATION

We, the declarant(s) (Pastors Name Here) as acting Overseer of Church Name Here, (Pastors Spouse) as a member of Church Name Here and Ordained (Pastors Name Here), declare and affirm the formation, organization and operation of, "New Church Name Here" as an association Church of Church Name Here is hereby petitioned for and authorized by we, the household heads, attesting by our signatures, hereunto, under penalties of perjury that the foregoing is true and correct. Executed on this ____ day of _____, 2013.

Signature_____Date:_____
Pursuant to 28 USC § 1746, I, (PASTORS NAME HERE), as Overseer of Church Name Here, Certify under penalty of perjury that all the foregoing information and statement(s) made above are true to the best of my knowledge.

State of_____
County of _____

Subscribed and sworn to (or affirmed) before me on this ____ day of _____, 2013 by (PASTORS NAME HERE), proved to me on the basis of satisfactory evidence to be the person(s) who appeared before me.

_____ (Seal)
Notary Public

Signature_____ Date:_____

Pursuant to 28 USC § 1746, I, (Pastors Spouse) as acting Church Member of Church Name Here, Certify under penalty of perjury that all the foregoing information and statement(s) made above are true to the best of my knowledge.

State of_____
County of _____

Subscribed and sworn to (or affirmed) before me on this ____ day of _____, 2013 by (Pastors Spouse), proved to me on the basis of satisfactory evidence to be the person(s) who appeared before me.

_____ (Seal)
Notary Public

Signature_____ Date:_____

Pursuant to 28 USC § 1746, I, Ordained (Pastors Name Here), acting as the newly ordained Pastor of New Church Name Here, Certify under penalty of perjury that all the foregoing information and statement(s) made above are true to the best of my knowledge.

State of_____
County of _____

Subscribed and sworn to (or affirmed) before me on this ____ day of _____, 2013 by Ordained (Pastors Name Here), proved to me on the basis of satisfactory evidence to be the person(s) who appeared before me.

Successor Trustee

_____ (Seal)
Notary Public

----------END OF ASSOCIATION CHURCH AND ORDINATION AFFIDAVIT----------------

As with the first affidavit, use the name change replacements in relationship to this 1st Amendment to the Association Church and Ordination Affidavit.

BEGIN 1st AMENDMENT TO THE ASSOCIATION CHURCH AND ORDINATION AFFIDAVIT:

PRESCRIBED SECOND AMENDMENT TO THE INTEGRATED AUXILIARIES AND CONVENTIONS OR ASSOCIATIONS OF CHURCHES AND ORDINATION OF MINISTRY LEADERSHIP UNDER THE AUTHORITY OF CHURCH NAME HERE AND *(PASTORS NAME HERE)* AS ACTING OVERSEER OF *(CHURCH NAME HERE)*

ASSIGNMENT OF SUCCESSOR AND SECRETARY TO NEW CHURCH NAME HERE PASTOR AND SUCCESSORS, A CORPORATION SOLE.

We, the undersigned declarant(s), on this _____ day of _____ in the Year of our Lord 20__, desiring to form and assign the positions of both, "Successor" and "Secretary" for our Association Church's Corporation Sole called, New Church Name Here Pastor and Successors, a Corporation Sole, hereby organize according to the following statute declaration(s) and article(s):

1. Successor. (Successor Person) is hereby named successor to the Office of, "Pastor" for New Church Name Here and to its Corporation Sole, which is named, New Church Name Here Pastor and successors, a corporation sole. In the event of the untimely death or resignation of

the, "Pastor" of New Church Name Here and its Corporation Sole, named, New Church Name Here Pastor and successors, a corporation sole, (Successor Person) shall inherit the title, all rights, holdings, financial accounts such as bank accounts (whether checking, savings, etc.), as well as brokerage or other investment accounts, real estate title(s) and deed(s) and any and all other forms of property, vehicles, equipment, supplies and privileges of "Pastor" for New Church Name Here and its Corporation Sole, New Church Name Here Pastor and successors, a corporation sole.

Signature_____ Date:_____
Pursuant to 28 U.S.C § 1746, I, (Successor Person), Successor, New Church Name Here Pastor and successors, a corporation sole. Certify under penalty of perjury that all the foregoing information and statement(s) made above are true to the best of my knowledge.

2. Secretary. (Secretary Person) is hereby named secretary of New Church Name Here Pastor and successors, a corporation sole.

Signature_____ Date:_____
Pursuant to 28 U.S.C § 1746, I, (Secretary Person), Secretary, Church Name Here Pastor and successors, a corporation sole. Certify under penalty of perjury that all the foregoing information and statement(s) made above are true to the best of my knowledge.

State of_____
County of _____

Subscribed and sworn to (or affirmed) before me on this ____ day of _____, 2013 by both (Successor Person) and (Secretary Person), proved to me on the basis of satisfactory evidence to be the person(s) who appeared before me.

_____ (Seal)
Notary Public

3. AUTHORIZATION

We, the declarant(s) Ordained (Pastors Name Here), (Successor Person) and (Secretary Person) declare the formation, organization and operation of the office and title position(s) of, "Successor", for New Church Name Here Pastor and successors, a corporation sole, and "Secretary", for New Church Name Here Pastor and successors, a corporation sole, are hereby petitioned for and authorized by we, the household heads, Church Leaders, attesting by our signatures, hereunto, under penalty of perjury that the foregoing is true and correct. Executed on this ____ day of _____, 2013.

Signature_____Date:_____
Pursuant to 28 U.S.C § 1746, I, Ordained (Pastors Name Here), Pastor, New Church Name Here Certify under penalty of perjury that all the foregoing information and statement(s) made above are true to the best of my knowledge.

State of_____
County of _____

Subscribed and sworn to (or affirmed) before me on this ____ day of _____, 2013 by Ordained (Pastors Name Here), proved to me on the basis of satisfactory evidence to be the person(s) who appeared before me.

_____ (Seal)
Notary Public

Signature_____ Date:_____

Pursuant to 28 U.S.C § 1746, I, (Successor Person), Church Member, Church Name Here Certify under penalty of perjury that all the foregoing information and statement(s) made above are true to the best of my knowledge.

State of_____
County of _____

Subscribed and sworn to (or affirmed) before me on this ____ day of _____, 2013 by (Successor Person), proved to me on the basis of satisfactory evidence to be the person(s) who appeared before me.

_____ (Seal)
Notary Public

Signature_____ Date:_____

Pursuant to 28 U.S.C § 1746, I, (Secretary Person), Church Member, Church Name Here Certify under penalty of perjury that all the foregoing information and statement(s) made above are true to the best of my knowledge.

State of_____
County of _____

Subscribed and sworn to (or affirmed) before me on this ____ day of _____, 2013 by (Secretary Person), proved to me on the basis of satisfactory evidence to be the person(s) who appeared before me.

_____ (Seal)
Notary Public

---------END OF 1st AMENDMENT TO THE ASSOCIATION
CHURCH AND ORDINATION AFFIDAVIT--------

These documents are exceptionally powerful and not to be used lightly. If you require us to act as your Association Church's Oregon based registered agent in order to help set up your Association Church's subsequent Corporation Sole, do not hesitate in filling out our online application here:
http://www.ChurchFreedom.org/apply.

CHAPTER 8 – A CALL TO ACTION!

I need to reiterate this scripture again:

Romans 8:18-21 declares, *"I consider that our present sufferings are not worth comparing with the glory that will be revealed in us. For the creation waits in eager expectation for the children of God to be revealed. For the creation was subjected to frustration, not by its own choice, but by the will of the one who subjected it, in hope that the creation itself will be liberated from its bondage to decay and brought into the freedom and glory of the children of God."* NIV

Do you understand the gravity to which this scripture mandates? This scripture is not limited in its description to the Earth but rather to ALL creation (meaning, the ENTIRE Universe). That, the Lord deliberately brought frustration and chaos to creation itself, in order that WE as the Children of God be revealed in hopes that WE can free the entirety of creation from bondage and decay and bring it into complete freedom and glory!! Amen?!

This is why bringing Godly order to the Church is so imperative and why we need your help. For all intents and purposes, this book contains nearly ALL the knowledge necessary to completely set up your Church, its subsequent Corporation Sole (with or without our help), Association Church, Ordain Pastors and even letters to challenge the IRS's inquires related to your exempt status. I would ask as a personal favor that you give this book to every single Christian Pastor (regardless of their denominational affiliation).

Time is of the essence! If we can help get the Body of Christ out from underneath the grip of 501c3 (even if it's only for a small season) at least that will give us some fighting chance to at least prepare and equip some saints for the coming time of calamity. With your help, we can bring forth Godly order BACK to the Body of Christ and eventually to ALL creation!

CHAPTER 9 – Church Establishment Affidavit.

Below, is our custom Church Affidavit. To download an editable version of this affidavit, please visit:

www.ChurchFreedom.org/donate

CHURCH ESTABLISHMENT AFFIDAVIT

We, the undersigned declarant(s), an assembly of Christian believers, on this _____ day of _____ in the Year of our Lord 20___, desiring to form together as a Church under the Lordship and Sovereignty of Jesus Christ, hereby organize according to the following statute declaration(s) and articles:

1. CHURCH NAME
   The name of this Church shall be, "CHURCH NAME HERE" (hereinafter referred to as "The Church").

2. GOVERNING DOCUMENTS
   Under the exclusive headship and sovereignty of the Lord Jesus Christ, the Church, its members, attendees, pastor(s), elder(s), deacon(s), etc., shall submit to and be governed in accordance with God's Word, the Holy Bible, as well as the Church's Constitution, Articles of Faith, and other governing documents which may from time to time be prescribed by the Church.

3. SCOPE OF POWERS
   The Church, acting through its Pastor(s), Elder(s), and any they may from time to time appoint, and pursuant to the Church's polity, shall be authorized to conduct Church activities and functions deemed necessary to the proper operation of the Church. Such activities shall include, but not be limited to, opening financial accounts such as bank accounts (whether checking, savings, etc.), as well as brokerage or other investment accounts, the purchase, lease or rental of church meeting facilities, as well as necessary office facilities, the purchase, lease or rental of church office equipment, musical instruments, sacerdotal accouterments, and any and all other forms of property, both real and personal, vehicles, equipment, supplies, implements or tools deemed necessary to the

proper operation of the Church, the purchase of insurance, the remuneration or compensation of the Church's minister(s) such as its pastor(s) and other ministers, the distribution of tangible and intangible gifts or benevolent charities, as well as any other necessary and appropriate financial transactions, the Church acting through its governing body, for the initiation, promotion, expansion and continuation of this ministry.

Current appointed and authorized Banking Checking or Savings Account Signatories are as follows:

Authorized Banking Signatory #1: PASTORS NAME HERE
Authorized Banking Signatory #2: PASTORS SPOUSE

4. TAX EXEMPT STATUS
   Pursuant to 26 USC § 508:

   (a) **New organizations must notify Secretary that they are applying for recognition of section 501(c)(3) status**
   Except as provided in subsection (c), an organization organized after October 9, 1969, shall not be treated as an organization described in section 501(c)(3)

   Specifically section 26 USC § 508(c)(1)(a), which reads,

   (c) **Exceptions**
   (1) **Mandatory exceptions**
   Subsections (a) and (b) shall not apply to—
   (A) churches, their integrated auxiliaries, and conventions or associations of churches

AND in reference to the Internal Revenue Code Publication 557 and IRC Publication section 501(c)(3), we, "The Church" formally declares that we are a **Tax Exempt Church** and as such, are **EXEMPT FROM FEDERAL INCOME TAX and are**

ELIGIBLE TO RECEIVE TAX DEDUCTIBLE CONTRIBUTIONS as Defined by both IRC Publication 557 and 501(c)(3), which states the following,

> **IRC PUBLICATION 557:** *"Organizations Not Required To File Form 1023*
>
> Some organizations **are not required** to file Form 1023. These include:
>
> **Churches**, interchurch organizations of local units of a church, conventions or associations of churches, or integrated auxiliaries of a church, such as a men's or women's organization, religious school, mission society, or youth group.
>
> **These organizations are <u>exempt automatically</u>** if they meet the requirements of section 501(c)(3)."
>
> **IRC Publication Section 501(c)(3) Definition of "Churches":**
> **Churches.** Although a church, its integrated auxiliaries, or a convention or association of churches **is not required to file Form 1023 to be exempt from federal income tax or to receive tax deductible contributions**, the organization may find it advantageous to obtain recognition of exemption.

We, "The Church" declare that we <u>DO NOT</u> find it 'advantageous' to 'obtain recognition of exemption' from the Internal Revenue Service as we respectfully retain and declare our sovereign right to remain a **Tax Exempt Church** as prescribed and described above and because the First Amendment of The Constitution of The United States of America clearly states, **"Congress shall make no law respecting an establishment of religion**, or prohibiting the free exercise thereof; or abridging the freedom of speech, or of the press; or the right of the people peaceably to assemble, and to petition the government for a redress of grievances."

We DECLARE and AFFIRM that we, "The Church" are

AUTOMATICALLY considered TAX EXEMPT from Federal Income Tax, Property Tax and that ALL Tithe and Offering contribution(s) shall be considered Tax Deductible pursuant to law.

5. DISTINCT LEGAL EXISTENCE

This affidavit serves to fulfill 28 USC § 1746 regarding sworn declarations under penalty of perjury. We, the declarant(s) PASTORS NAME HERE, PASTORS SPOUSE, WITNESS #1 and WITNESS #2 declare and recognize the distinct lawful existence of CHURCH NAME HERE as a bona fide Church.

6. RECOGNIZED CREED AND FORM OF WORSHIP

We, the declarant(s) PASTORS NAME HERE, PASTORS SPOUSE, WITNESS #1 and WITNESS #2 declare, affirm that CHURCH NAME HERE has a recognized creed and form of worship through our faith in Jesus Christ. We believe the Bible to be the inspired, infallible, authoritative Word of God. We believe in the deity of our Lord Jesus Christ, in His virgin birth, in His sinless life, in His miracles, in His vicarious and atoning death through His shed blood, in His bodily resurrection, in His ascension to the right hand of the Father, and in His personal return in power and glory.

7. DEFINITE AND DISTINCT ECCLESIASTICAL GOVERNMENT

We, the declarant(s) PASTORS NAME HERE, PASTORS SPOUSE, WITNESS #1 and WITNESS #2 declare and affirm that Jesus Christ holds supreme authority as the chief priest of the Church and that his Holy Spirit shall act as the supreme authority of our ecclesiastical government.

8. FORMAL CODE OF DOCTRINE AND DISCIPLINE

We, the declarant(s) PASTORS NAME HERE, PASTORS SPOUSE, WITNESS #1 and WITNESS #2 declare, affirm and recognize four distinct doctrines:

5. Salvation Through Jesus Christ.
6. The Manifestation of the Divine Gifts of the Spirit (as Described in 1st Corinthians 12).
7. Upon being born again, our salvation is sealed with the baptism of the Holy Spirit.
8. The Second Coming of Jesus Christ.

We also believe and practice three ordinances:

4. Water Baptism by Immersion after repenting of one's sins and receiving Christ's gift of salvation.
5. Holy Communion (the Lord's Supper) as a symbolic remembrance of Christ's suffering and death for our salvation.
6. That we make every effort to do what leads to peace and mutual edification for ALL members in the Body of Christ.

9. DISTINCT RELIGIOUS HISTORY

We, the declarant(s) PASTORS NAME HERE, PASTORS SPOUSE, WITNESS #1 and WITNESS #2 declare and affirm that the genesis of the distinct religious history of CHURCH NAME HERE started with The Bible and that this Church Establishment Affidavit serves as a continued testament to the legitimacy of it's historical legacy.

10. MEMBERSHIP NOT ASSOCIATED WITH ANY OTHER CHURCH OR DENOMINATION

We, the declarant(s) PASTORS NAME HERE, PASTORS SPOUSE, WITNESS #1 and WITNESS #2 affirm that membership to CHURCH NAME HERE is not associated with any other Church or Denomination outside of the Christian Faith.

11. ORGANIZATION OF ORDAINED MINISTER(S) AND ORDAINED MINISTER(S) SELECTED AFTER COMPLETING PRESCRIBED STUDIES

We, the declarant(s) PASTORS SPOUSE, WITNESS #1 and WITNESS #2 declare, affirm that PASTORS NAME HERE has completed a competent amount of biblical studies and is hereby ordained as Senior Pastor of CHURCH NAME HERE. PASTORS SPOUSE shall act as Sr. Associate Pastor and WITNESS #2 as Associate Pastor. Apart of the responsibilities of the office of "Pastor" here at CHURCH NAME HERE will be to conduct religious ceremonies such as officiating marriage, conducting baptisms, issuing certificates on behalf of the Church, ministering the gospel, teaching, prophesying, delivering messages of wisdom, imparting knowledge, exercising the gift of healing, expressing faith, exercising miracles, signs and wonders, exercising discernment of the distinguishing of spirits, speaking in different kinds of tongues and using the gift of interpretation for the edification of the body of believers.

12. CHURCH – LITERATURE OF ITS OWN

We, the declarant(s) PASTORS NAME HERE, PASTORS SPOUSE, WITNESS #1 and WITNESS #2 declare and affirm that this Church Establishment Affidavit and its various statements of CHURCH NAME HERE's faith, doctrines and ordinances shall be publically known and will serve as literature of its own accord.

13. ESTABLISHED PLACE(S) OF WORSHIP, REGULAR CONGREGATION(S) AND REGULAR RELIGIOUS SERVICES

We, the declarant(s) PASTORS NAME HERE, PASTORS SPOUSE, WITNESS #1 and WITNESS #2 declare and affirm as a regular fellowship of believers that CHURCH NAME HERE holds regular services for the empowerment and spiritual equipping for the benefit to the Body of Christ. We affirm and declare that the specific meeting places for these times of worship may vary to locations such as a leased or owned building or house, public property, meeting halls, restaurants, coffee shops, radio communications, conference call, cell phone conversations, online webinar(s), social media platforms, forums and all forms of digital communications (such as but not limited to website domains) that allow for the gathering of members of "The Church".

14. RELIGIOUS INSTRUCTION OF THE YOUNG

We, the declarant(s) PASTORS NAME HERE, PASTORS SPOUSE, WITNESS #1 and WITNESS #2 declare and affirm the practice of instructing the young in the ways of the Lord.

15. PREPARATION FOR MINISTER(S)

We, the declarant(s) PASTORS NAME HERE, PASTORS SPOUSE, WITNESS #1 and WITNESS #2 declare and affirm that if a member of CHURCH NAME HERE desires to become an ordained minister, that they must have their house in Godly order as described in 1st Timothy Chapter Three. 1st Timothy Chapter Three shall serve as a guide to being qualified for ordination here at CHURCH NAME HERE. Ordination shall be prescribed only by the discretion of authorized Church personal such as PASTORS NAME HERE as acting Senior Pastor.

16. SAME SEX MARRIAGE IS STRICTLY PROHIBITED AND AFFIRMATION(S) AND DECLARATION(S) AGAINST THE LESBIAN, GAY, BI-SEXUAL, TRANSGENDERED AND HOMOSEXUAL LIFESTYLE AND EMPLOYEE, VOLUNTEER AND APOINTMENT RESTRICTIONS TO HOMOSEXUAL, BI-SEXUAL AND TRANSGENDERED PERSON(S) AND PROHIBITED USE OF FACILITIES TO HOMOSEXUAL AND TRANSGENDERED INDIVIDUALS.

We, the declarant(s) PASTORS NAME HERE, PASTORS SPOUSE, WITNESS #1 and WITNESS #2 declare and affirm that it is against our religious beliefs to conduct same sex marriage, celebrate nor perform same sex unions. We hereby declare and affirm that marriage is solely to be between a man and a woman for the purposes of producing godly offspring as declared in the infallible word of God spoken through the prophet Malachi in the book of Malachi 2:15-16 which declares, " Has not the one God made you? You belong to him in body and spirit. And what does the one God seek? **Godly offspring**. So be on your guard, and do not be unfaithful to the wife of your youth. "The man who hates and divorces his wife," says the Lord, the God of Israel, "does violence to the one he should protect," says the Lord Almighty. So be on your guard, and do not be unfaithful.

Furthermore, we declare and affirm that the practice of the homosexual, bi-sexual and transgendered lifestyle to be detestable before the Lord and those practicing such act(s) and behavior(s) will not inherit the Kingdom of Heaven. This is in accordance with Gods Holy word as described in Leviticus 18:22, Leviticus 20:13, Romans 1:27 and 1st Corinthians 6:9.

Leviticus 18:22 states, "Do not have sexual relations with a man as one does with a woman; that is detestable."

Leviticus 20:13 states, "If a man has sexual relations with a man as one does with a woman, both of them have done what is detestable. They are to be put to death; their blood will be on their own heads."

Romans 1:27 states, "In the same way the men also abandoned natural relations with women and were inflamed with lust for one another. Men committed shameful acts with other men, and received in themselves the due penalty for their error."

1st Corinthians 6:9 states, "Or do you not know that wrongdoers will not inherit the kingdom of God? Do not be deceived: Neither the sexually immoral nor idolaters nor adulterers nor men who have sex with men."

Furthermore, we declare and affirm our religious right to deny membership, volunteer assignments, appointments and employment to anyone that is actively involved with or condones the Lesbian, Gay, Bi-Sexual, Transgendered and Homosexual Lifestyle.

Furthermore, we declare and affirm that the use of any church owned facility may only be used for weddings that adhere to the traditional

Biblical definition of marriage between a man and a woman and are solely reserved for use by members and their immediate family members of our same belief and not to same sex couples, gays, lesbians or transgendered person(s). These facilities may not be used by any individual, group, or organization that advocate, endorse, or promote homosexuality as an alternative or acceptable lifestyle. This policy also applies to birthday parties, reunions, anniversaries, wedding or baby showers, etc. Under no circumstances is the pastor, or any affiliate of this church, to officiate, participate, or endorse any wedding ceremony that violates the belief and teaching of this church body in accordance with the Bible.

The Lord has also decreed that no activity of our Church shall be dictated too nor governed by Local, State or Federal authorities that shall supersede our religious freedom(s), Liberties and Right(s) in accordance with our affirmation(s) and declaration(s) as outlined in this section 16.

17. AUTHORIZATION

We, the declarant(s), PASTORS NAME HERE, PASTORS SPOUSE, WITNESS #1 and WITNESS #2 declare the formation, organization and operation of, "The Church" is hereby petitioned for and authorized by we, the household heads, attesting by our signatures, hereunto, under penalty of perjury that the foregoing is true and correct. Executed upon the signing of this affidavit.

Signature_____Date:_____ Title:
PASTOR
Pursuant to 28 USC § 1746, I, PASTORS NAME HERE, As Senior Pastor, CHURCH NAME HERE

Certify under penalty of perjury that all the foregoing information and statement(s) made above are true to the best of my knowledge.

State of_____
County of_____

Subscribed and sworn to (or affirmed) before me on this ____ day of _____, ____ by PASTORS NAME HERE, proved to me on the basis of satisfactory evidence to be the person(s) who appeared before me.

_____ (Seal)
Notary Public

Signature_____ Date:_____
Pursuant to 28 USC § 1746, I, PASTORS SPOUSE, As Senior Associate Pastor, CHURCH NAME HERE. Certify under penalty of perjury that all the foregoing information and statement(s) made above are true to the best of my knowledge.

State of_____
County of_____

Subscribed and sworn to (or affirmed) before me on this ____ day of _____, ____ by PASTORS SPOUSE, proved to me on the basis of satisfactory evidence to be the person(s) who appeared before me.

_____ (Seal)

Notary Public

Signature_____ Date:_____
Pursuant to 28 USC § 1746, I, WITNESS #1, Church Member, CHURCH NAME HERE Certify under penalty of perjury that all the foregoing information and statement(s) made above are true to the best of my knowledge.

State of_____
County of _____

Subscribed and sworn to (or affirmed) before me on this ____ day of _____, ____ by WITNESS #1, proved to me on the basis of satisfactory evidence to be the person(s) who appeared before me.

_____ (Seal)
Notary Public

Signature_____ Date:_____
Pursuant to 28 USC § 1746, I, WITNESS #2, Associate Pastor, CHURCH NAME HERE Certify under penalty of perjury that all the foregoing information and statement(s) made above are true to the best of my knowledge.

State of_____
County of _____

Subscribed and sworn to (or affirmed) before me on this ____ day of _____, ____ by WITNESS #2, proved to me on the basis of satisfactory evidence to be the person(s) who appeared before me.

_____ (Seal)
Notary Public

PRESCRIBED FIRST AMENDMENT TO THE CHURCH ESTABLISHMENT AFFIDAVIT

ASSIGNMENT OF THE OFFICE OF "OVERSEER" TO CHURCH NAME HERE AND EXEMPTION FROM FILING ANNUAL INFORMATION RETURNS TO THE INTERNAL REVENUE SERVICE, MANDATORY EXEMPTION STATUS AS RECOGNIZED IN FEDERAL LAW, DECLARATION(S) REGARDING VARIOUS RELIGIOUS FREEDOMS OF EXPRESSION AND SPEECH AND DECLARATION OF JURISDICTIONAL AUTHORITIES WITHIN THE CHURCH.

We, the undersigned declarant(s), on this _____ day of _____ in the Year of our Lord _____, desiring to form the Office of "Overseer" for CHURCH NAME HERE, hereby organize according to the following declaration(s) and article(s):

1. ASSIGNMENT OF THE LIMITED AND ISOLATED CORPORATION SOLE TITLE AND OFFICE OF OVERSEER

It is hereby appointed that PASTORS NAME HERE, as acting senior pastor of CHURCH NAME HERE, shall now be given an additional Office and Title of, "Overseer" for CHURCH NAME HERE. The purpose(s) and limitation(s) of the authority(s) granted this isolated Corporation Sole office and title position within the Church is to solely manage and distribute Church related financial asset(s) and holding(s) and act as an individual and natural person in all Church related financial transactions. This title of "Overseer" shall not associate with the other title and position of "Senior Pastor" and shall be a separate office unto itself. The Title and Office of "Overseer" serves no other function, nor has any other additional authorities outside of managing and distributing Church related financial assets, holdings and act as a natural person in all Church related financial transaction(s).

2. MANDATORY EXEMPTION FROM FILING ANNUAL INFORMATION RETURNS TO THE INTERNAL REVENUE SERVICE, MANDATORY EXEMPTION STATUS AS RECOGNIZED IN FEDERAL LAW AND DECLARATION(S) REGARDING VARIOUS RELIGIOUS FREEDOMS OF EXPRESSION AND SPEECH

We, the declarant(s) PASTORS NAME HERE, PASTORS SPOUSE, WITNESS #1 and WITNESS #2 declare and affirm that pursuant to 26 USC § 6033(3)(A)(1-3), which states,

(3) **Exceptions from filing**
(A) **Mandatory exceptions**
Paragraph (1) shall not apply to—
(i) *churches, their integrated auxiliaries, and conventions or associations of churches*,
(ii) any organization (other than a private foundation, as defined in section 509 (a)) described in subparagraph (C), the gross receipts of which in each taxable year are normally not more than $5,000, or
(iii) *the exclusively religious activities of any religious order.*

That our Church, CHURCH NAME HERE and it's subsequent Corporation Sole, CHURCH NAME HERE OVERSEER are MANDATORILY exempted from filing annual information returns to the Internal Revenue Service and that all of the operations, financial or otherwise, related to CHURCH NAME HERE's subsequent Corporation Sole, CHURCH NAME HERE OVERSEER, shall be considered the exclusively religious activities of the religious order, which is the Corporation Sole itself within the Church and is thus mandatorily exempted from filing annual information returns to the IRS.

We, the declarant(s), also affirm and declare that the office of the Corporation Sole shall act as a natural person in all ministry related transaction(s) or dealing(s) and that all dealing(s) done on behalf of the Corporation Sole, are to the benefit, growth and operation of The

Church and any individual member(s) of the Church. Our authority to declare the Corporation Sole acting as a natural person is affirmed in the Internal Revenue Service's **Internal Revenue Bulletin: 2004-12, March 22, 2004, Rev. Rul. 2004-27 presently located at http://www.irs.gov/irb/2004-12_IRB/ar11.html** which states, *"A corporation sole may own property and enter into contracts as a **<u>natural person</u>**, but only for the purposes of the religious entity and not for the individual office holder's personal benefit."*

Sometimes a Church must appropriate resources, donated through the fellowship of believers, which will directly impact or benefit any individual(s) that are associated with the Church. We recognize that currently there is no Federal or State law that prohibit(s) a Church from appropriating or allocating funds given to the Church, by a tithing member, in any manner the Church deems necessary for the continuity and continued function of the Church and its fellowship.

In fact, with keeping with the Royal Law of Heaven that states in Luke 10:27, *"'Love the Lord your God with all your heart and with all your soul and with all your strength and with all your mind'; and, 'Love your neighbor as yourself.'"*

And with keeping the principles of Romans 14:19, which states, *"Let us therefore make every effort to do what leads to peace and to mutual edification."*

And with keeping the principles of Acts 2:44-47, which states, *"All the believers were together and had everything in common. They sold property and possessions to give to anyone who had need. Every day they continued to meet together in the temple courts. They broke bread in their homes and ate together with glad and sincere hearts, praising God and enjoying the favor of all the people. And the Lord added to their number daily those who were being saved."*

And with keeping the principles of 1st John 3:17, which states, *"If anyone has material possessions and sees a brother or sister in need but has no pity on them, how can the love of God be in that person?"*

We, declare and affirm it to be our religious freedom of speech to use any means of the financial resource(s) gifted or donated to CHURCH NAME HERE or it's Corporation Sole, CHURCH NAME HERE OVERSEER, to be distributed as the Holy Spirit commands for the personal use and personal benefit of any individual(s) the Church deems necessary to have that favor as a member or non-member of the Church in the hope that the Lord adds to our number daily those who were being saved. This is a command given to us by The Lord of Heaven and therefor a religious duty to be exercised according to our religious rights and liberties.

Furthermore, we the declarant(s), would like to stand on the following legal definition(s), case precedent(s) and benefit(s) regarding our Corporation Sole acting as a 'Natural Person':

Firstly, we agree with the definition of a "natural person" and an "individual" as defined by Blacks Law Dictionary 9th Edition as:

Person *(Be) 1. A human being. Also termed natural person.*
Individual*, adj. (I5c) 1. Existing as an indivisible entity. 2. For relating to a single person or thing, as opposed to a group.*

We recognize that these two definition(s) are identical in nature to one another and are related to each other in every way possible.

Furthermore, we also recognize The United States Supreme Court Ruling of Hale v. Henkel, 201 U.S. 43 (1906) in which then Supreme Court Chief Justice Melville Fuller stated,

"The individual may stand upon his constitutional Rights as a citizen. He is entitled to carry on his private business in his own way. His power to contract is unlimited. He owes no such duty [to submit his books and papers for an examination] to the State, since he receives nothing therefrom, beyond the protection of his life and property. His Rights are such as existed by the law of the land [Common Law] long antecedent to the organization of the State, and can only be taken from him by due process of law, and in accordance with the Constitution. Among his Rights are a refusal to incriminate himself, and the immunity of himself and his property from arrest or seizure except under a warrant of the law. He owes

nothing to the public so long as he does not trespass upon their Rights."

Because both the court(s) and the IRS define the Corporation Sole as a 'Natural Person' in all business related transaction(s) or dealing(s) on behalf of the Church, it never relinquishes it's lawful right to be continually viewed as its own independent individual, wielding authority as a natural person and not looked as a corporate creature of fiction. We declare that this gives the Corporation Sole the same authority(s), right(s) and privilege(s) as the individual has, as defined by Supreme Court Chief Justice Melville Fuller, unless otherwise proven differently in a Federal Court of law by a Jury of our peers.

3. DECLARATION OF JURISDICTIONAL AUTHORITIES WITHIN THE CHURCH

We, the declarant(s) PASTORS NAME HERE, PASTORS SPOUSE, WITNESS #1 and WITNESS #2 declare and affirm that there are many title(s) and office(s) held within CHURCH NAME HERE. When teaching or giving instructions to the congregation or the public, PASTORS NAME HERE will only be acting in the position, title and office of the Senior Pastor and NOT the office of the Corporation Sole known as CHURCH NAME HERE OVERSEER. The title and office of Overseer and the Corporation Sole shall be limited to overseeing the Churches financial asset(s), obligation(s), title(s) to real property(s), title(s) to vehicle(s) owned by the Church and shall be the religious order within the Church that is directly responsible for conducting the exclusively religious activities on behalf of the Church.

4. AUTHORIZATION

We, the declarant(s), PASTORS NAME HERE, PASTORS SPOUSE, WITNESS #1 and WITNESS #2, declare the formation, organization and operation of the office and title position(s) of,

"Overseer" of CHURCH NAME HERE, the Corporation Sole's mandatory exemption from filing, the Corporation Sole's authority to perpetually act as an individual and natural person in the execution of it's official duties and we declare the distinct jurisdictional authorities between the title and office of the Senior Pastor position within the Church from that of the Title and Office of the Overseer position and are hereby petitioned for and authorized by we, the household heads, Church Members, attesting by our signatures, using our constitutionally protected religious freedom of expression hereunto, under penalty of perjury that the foregoing is true and correct. Executed upon the signing of this affidavit.

Signature_____Date:_____ Title:
PASTOR
Pursuant to 28 USC § 1746, I, PASTORS NAME HERE, Senior Pastor, CHURCH NAME HERE, Certify under penalty of perjury that all the foregoing information and statement(s) made above are true to the best of my knowledge.

State of_____
County of _____

Subscribed and sworn to (or affirmed) before me on this ____ day of _____, ____ by PASTORS NAME HERE, proved to me on the basis of satisfactory evidence to be the person(s) who appeared before me.

_____ (Seal)
Notary Public

Signature_____ Date:_____

Pursuant to 28 USC § 1746, I, PASTORS SPOUSE, Senior Associate Pastor, CHURCH NAME HERE OVERSEER. Certify under penalty of perjury that all the foregoing information and statement(s) made above are true to the best of my knowledge.

State of_____
County of _____

Subscribed and sworn to (or affirmed) before me on this ____ day of _____, ____ by PASTORS SPOUSE, proved to me on the basis of satisfactory evidence to be the person(s) who appeared before me.

_____ (Seal)
Notary Public

Signature_____ Date:_____
Pursuant to 28 USC § 1746, I, WITNESS #1, Church Member, CHURCH NAME HERE Certify under penalty of perjury that all the foregoing information and statement(s) made above are true to the best of my knowledge.

State of_____
County of _____

Subscribed and sworn to (or affirmed) before me on this ____ day of _____, ____ by WITNESS #1, proved to me on the basis of satisfactory evidence to be the person(s) who appeared before me.

_____ (Seal)
Notary Public

Signature_____ Date:_____
Pursuant to 28 USC § 1746, I, WITNESS #2, Associate Pastor, CHURCH NAME HERE Certify under penalty of perjury that all the foregoing information and statement(s) made above are true to the best of my knowledge.

State of_____
County of _____

Subscribed and sworn to (or affirmed) before me on this ____ day of _____, ____ by WITNESS #2, proved to me on the basis of satisfactory evidence to be the person(s) who appeared before me.

_____ (Seal)
Notary Public

PRESCRIBED SECOND AMENDMENT TO THE CHURCH ESTABLISHMENT AFFIDAVIT

ASSIGNMENT OF SUCCESSOR AND SECRETARY TO CHURCH NAME HERE OVERSEER.

We, the undersigned declarant(s), on this _____ day of _____ in the Year of our Lord _____, desiring to form and assign the positions of both, "Successor" and "Secretary" for our Church's Corporation Sole called, CHURCH NAME HERE OVERSEER, hereby organize according to the following statute declaration(s) and article(s):

18. Successor. SUCCESSOR NAME HERE is hereby named successor to the Office of, "Overseer" for CHURCH NAME HERE and to its Corporation Sole, which is named, CHURCH NAME HERE OVERSEER. In the event of the untimely death or resignation of the, "Overseer" of CHURCH NAME HERE and its Corporation Sole, named, CHURCH NAME HERE OVERSEER, SUCCESSOR NAME HERE shall inherit the title, all rights, holdings, financial accounts such as bank accounts (whether checking, savings, etc.), as well as brokerage or other investment accounts, real estate title(s) and deed(s) and any and all other forms of property, vehicles, equipment, supplies and privileges of "Overseer" for CHURCH NAME HERE and it's Corporation Sole, CHURCH NAME HERE OVERSEER.

Signature_____ Date:_____
Pursuant to 28 USC § 1746, I, SUCCESSOR NAME HERE, Successor to Corporation Sole for CHURCH NAME HERE OVERSEER. Certify under penalty of perjury that all the foregoing information and statement(s) made above are true to the best of my knowledge.

State of_____
County of _____

Subscribed and sworn to (or affirmed) before me on this ____ day of _____, ____ by SUCCESSOR NAME HERE, proved to me on the basis of satisfactory evidence to be the person(s) who appeared before me.

_____ (Seal)
Notary Public

19. Secretary. SECRETARY NAME HERE is hereby named secretary of CHURCH NAME HERE OVERSEER.

Signature_____ Date:_____
Pursuant to 28 USC § 1746, I, SECRETARY NAME HERE, Secretary, CHURCH NAME HERE OVERSEER. Certify under penalty of perjury that all the foregoing information and statement(s) made above are true to the best of my knowledge.

State of_____
County of _____

Subscribed and sworn to (or affirmed) before me on this ____ day of _____, ____ by SECRETARY NAME HERE, proved to me on the basis of satisfactory evidence to be the person(s) who appeared before me.

_____ (Seal)
Notary Public

20. AUTHORIZATION

We, the declarant(s), PASTORS NAME HERE, PASTORS SPOUSE and WITNESS #1 declare the formation, organization and operation of the office and title position(s) of, "Successor", for CHURCH NAME HERE OVERSEER, and "Secretary", for CHURCH NAME HERE OVERSEER, are hereby petitioned for and authorized by we, the household heads, Church Members, attesting by our signatures, hereunto, under penalty of perjury that the foregoing is true and correct. Executed on this ____ day of _____, ____.

Signature_____Date:_____
Pursuant to 28 USC § 1746, I, PASTORS NAME HERE, As Senior Pastor and Overseer, CHURCH NAME HERE Certify under penalty of perjury that all the foregoing information and statement(s) made above are true to the best of my knowledge.

State of_____
County of _____

Subscribed and sworn to (or affirmed) before me on this ____ day of _____, ____ by PASTORS NAME HERE, proved to me on the basis of satisfactory evidence to be the person(s) who appeared before me.

_____ (Seal)
Notary Public

Signature_____ Date:_____
Pursuant to 28 USC § 1746, I, WITNESS #1, Church Member, CHURCH NAME HERE Certify under penalty of perjury that all the foregoing information and statement(s) made above are true to the best of my knowledge.

State of_____
County of_____

Subscribed and sworn to (or affirmed) before me on this ____ day of _____, ____ by WITNESS #1, proved to me on the basis of satisfactory evidence to be the person(s) who appeared before me.

_____ (Seal)
Notary Public

Signature_____ Date:_____
Pursuant to 28 USC § 1746, I, PASTORS SPOUSE, Senior Associate Pastor, CHURCH NAME HERE Certify under penalty of perjury that all the foregoing information and statement(s) made above are true to the best of my knowledge.

State of_____
County of_____

Subscribed and sworn to (or affirmed) before me on this ____ day of _____, ____ by PASTORS SPOUSE, proved to me on the basis of satisfactory evidence to be the person(s) who appeared before me.

_____ (Seal)
Notary Public

TO CONTACT JOSHUA KENNY-GREENWOOD OR THE EMPOWERMENT CENTER

Please help support our cause of helping to set Churches FREE from 501c3! Send your religious item donation to the following:
Web Site: **www.ChurchFreedom.org/Donate**

YouTube Ministry:
www.youtube.com/user/EmpowermentCenter1

Facebook Ministry:
www.facebook.com/CorporationSole

and

www.TestimonyToday.org

Weekly Sermons Through SoundCloud:
www.soundcloud.com/ChurchFreedom

To apply for us to support you in setting up both your Church/ministry and Corporation Sole, please go to:
www.ChurchFreedom.org/apply

Contact Us/Support Email:
www.ChurchFreedom.org/Support

NOTES:

Pastoral Reviews and Endorsements:

If knowledge is power then the knowledge acted upon that you will receive from this new dynamic eye-opening book will birth a new and fresh you in ministry. The knowledge, information and existence of the corporation sole is not new it's just not been taught. The Lord has called men like Joshua to bring forth this knowledge with facts and references for you to quickly learn and start to adapt to make the changes you need to do your job effectively and to prosper your ministry.

For years I questioned why powerful men and women of God seemed to dodge the hard issues regarding the times we live in. One of the main reasons is due to the current restrictions and limitations imposed by 501c3. Churches all across our beloved country are bound by what can be said and done in the pulpit to further the cause of Christ and His people.

If you are ready to preach unleashed then setting your ministry free with the corporation sole is the answer you've been seeking. Change is inevitable and once you've tasted the information in this book you can't go back to ministry business as usual.

I encourage you to study this book, pray as you study this book and desire to hear from the Spirit of God yourself as to what He would have you do.

With a corporation sole and the proper set-up of your ministry I consider that as part of getting your house in order.
May the Holy Spirit continue to enlighten you in all things and may you stay faithful to your call in these challenging times, these difficult times yet it's always harvest time!
Enjoy your blessings!

—Pastor Thomas Clark, Spirit of Truth Ministries, Gardena, California.

Overseer Joshua Kenny Greenwood has truly heard from Heaven in the creation of this book. Having been personally responsible for helping more than 50 churches qualify for 501(c)3 status, I was overjoyed to discover the truths that Joshua has placed within the pages of this book. This review is insufficient for the expression of my estimation of this book's value to the Kingdom of God. I have no doubt that every Spiritual Leader called by God to start a ministry in this country, needs to get a copy of this book. I will be sowing copies into the lives of all of the ministry leaders in covenant with me in this country. This book signals a shift to true liberty for the Body of Christ in America. Grace to You Joshua.
---Bishop Walter Roberts, Heal the Nations, North Carolina

Pastor and Overseer, Joshua Greenwood has encapsulated GOD's "Present Times" Shift giving blueprint, to every Pastor with ears to hear, on how to subdue that which JESUS the CHRIST of Nazareth has already redeemed via the Corporation Sole.

No longer can the church afford to continue its starring role in "Silence of the Lambs" fostering a People of GOD without power or authority to effectuate KINGDOM authority on earth.

Joshua has candidly released GOD's TRUTH into the atmosphere, shedding a bright light on that which darkness for far too long perpetrated through 501(c)3 incorporated state churches; whereby, giving American churches a "form" of godliness-having no power to do the works of the KINGDOM, as purposed by GOD, in every sphere of influence in American society

Brilliantly written, Joshua takes the guess work out of "Getting Your Church House in Order" by giving step by step guide on how to come OUT from amongst them and give voice to GOD's clarion call; for the trumpet has been blown in Zion.

---Bridgette Chapman, Overseer, Christian Conservatory Prep Overseer and Successors, A Corporation Sole, Long Island, New York

Wow! Zam! Pow! Once again The Empowerment Center and Joshua Greenwood have exploded into the enemy's camp and have taken no prisoners. The multi-layered, magnified and multiplied lies of the evil one have been laid bare for all to see while the path to freedom shines brighter and brighter for the righteous until the full day! (Prov. 4:18 NASB) Clear, concise, easy to read and understand, Mr. Greenwood takes a potentially complex issue and provides concrete steps to enable anyone to do what God has called them to do. This book will undoubtedly be included in the short list of books that produced a major paradigm shift in the modern day Body of Christ. I highly recommend that everyone who desires to impact the world, along with all those in their sphere of influence, obtain this book and put it into practice. It's time to "render unto Caesar that what is Caesar's and unto God what is God's". Let's come out from under the control and influence of the spirit of this world and take our stand beside our God as the kingdoms of this world become the kingdoms of our Lord and of His Christ.

---Gene Rayle, Overseer of Blue Skies Ministries in High Point, North Carolina

As Founding Church Pastor, I have been frustrated and concerned with the uninvolvement of the church, concerning the state of our nation. Where is the voice of this giant called 'the church'? What intimidation was strong enough to silence US?
Many good men and woman, from different denominations or non-denominations, believers in- and disciples of- Christ, are not speaking out against ungodliness and immorality, against leaders and people placed in authority who have evil hearts and motives! Why are Christians and Churches not exposing corruption in government, the FDA, the IRS, the NSA etc. Why are we as Americans threatened to the extent of not exercising our freedom of speech? ... THE ANSWER IS "FEAR"! Fear of imprisonment, fear of being targeted by for example the IRS, Fear of being dragged to

court and sued with heavy fines, even imprisonment. That Fear is a spirit that's not from God. As I read and continue to read this very informative, detailed and revelatory work, my own fears were exposed and defeated. Although it sounds new, I'm shocked to learn that it's 'old news' that was withheld from the Church and the Christian believers. The moral 'Christian Church' backbone of this great nation have been lulled and deceived into silence, through Fear of persecution, convinced that we must submit to and obey government first and then God last. This highly informative and detailed work guide is giving the Christian Church and believer the knowledge we need to not be deceived nor destroyed any further! Hosea 4:6 My people are destroyed (cut off) through a lack of knowledge. I believe that this manual is JUST IN TIME, to raise up the Christian believer and Church to preach the Gospel like never before. We can only do this as Free Moral and Loving followers of Christ. Invest whatever it takes immediately, to empower yourself and your Church and fellow Christian believers, and get this manual on your desk, next to your Bible. Sow a seed in more copies and share this with every Pastor and every believer in Christ whom you know. If you continue in the truth... then you shall know the truth, and the truth shall make you free! Thank you Overseer Joshua, for being an anointed and bold voice to this generation. I am one of millions to come, who is and will be forever grateful for what you stand for and teach. God will expand your territory of influence and the Gospel will be preached like never before.

---Pieter van Dyk, Pastor of New Creation Church in Houston, Texas

This book is so exciting! It got me riled up right away when Josh said, "lets stop complaining and start taking over!" That's how I think! From that point on it was an easy read and my heart was pounding. Besides the laws, he explains how the government has come to literally own and enslave the church, and how to FREE ourselves, which is our DIVINE RIGHT! That is exactly what Jesus wanted for us. This book is a must for everyone who owns a corporation sole. It helped me understand how my Church is structured, how to avoid making horrible mistakes, how to set up the business of the Church and more. The education and painstaking research Josh shares, how to do everything for your corporation sole, even how to form your own corporation sole or what to do if the IRS comes knocking, how to avoid accidentally destroying your Church and Corporation Sole, is within these pages. READ IT!!!

---Sarah Roberts, Overseer of World Church in Van Nuys, California

It is a privilege to be a Reviewer of this very important Book entitled "The Corporation Sole Freeing America's Pulpits and ENDING the Restrictive 501c3 Laws for Churches" by Joshua Kenny-Greenwood. The church cannot serve two masters especially when Christ tells them to be salt and preserve society and the IRS tells them to stay out of the political arena and become irrelevant - which they have done. Having obeyed the IRS rather than the Bible, they have become irrelevant, savorless salt, good for nothing but tyranny - which they have allowed to come upon them and the rest of the country by their inaction. The church in America had the power to hold the government accountable to a higher law that prevented corruption. It has forfeited its power by disobeying the direct commands and warnings of Jesus. Consequently, the civil powers are well on their way to corruption, tyranny and enthroning themselves as the highest authority - above God and above the will of the people themselves. The civil authorities have become masters rather than servants.

The solution is straightforward although not simple. (Anything that involves pride on the one hand, and disentanglement from government bureaucracies on the other, will not be simple.) I encourage every Christian, every Pastor to join me take action:

1. Get churches out from under the suppression of the State and IRS - Unlicensed them, free them. Make them sovereign so they can protect freedom for all, as obtained at the founding of this country - we are not talking "theocracy". This will also bring them back under the protection of the first amendment of the constitution. As non-profit corporations they are not protected by the first amendment.

2. *Get Christian congregations back into the marketplace of ideas and the peaceful political processes that have gotten so corrupt without their presence. These processes were set up by predominantly Christian founders to alleviate the necessity of shedding blood in the turnover of public servants!*

Mr. Greenwood has answered my question - using the Bible, using the history of corporations and the American church, using his in-depth following of case law in this area, and finally by using his experience from hands-on work with hundreds of churches trying to become unlicensed. The depth of research and originality of perspective is astounding. I learned through looking at the history of the church in our country that it was not always so meek and timid. In fact, Americans owe their freedom to the Biblical political philosophy of freedom, which was propounded from the pulpit to the enlightenment of the founding era citizenry.

But that was a different church. Today's church could be salty, could preserve freedom, could help inject salty Christians into the political system to preserve against corruption - if it would take to heart Jesus' warnings and commands and jettison its voluntarily chosen, new masters, the State and the IRS.

Greenwood is thoroughly involved in the solution to the problem. His organization, The Empowerment Center has a Training Series and other tools online that goes into detail on the right way to become an unlicensed free church. His book pointed out a piercing but simple observation:
Consider that incorporated churches that have `employees' rather than `ministry workers' have become tax collectors (publicans) for the State! They collect payroll and withholding taxes for the State and IRS. This revelation shocked me because it is hidden in plain

sight. It is so obvious, so accepted, and such a strong clue that something is terribly wrong with the church-state relationship - yet church members are oblivious to it. Where in the Bible has Jesus even hinted that His Church, His Body on earth, His Bride, should collect taxes for the civil government? Is this also not being unequally yoked?

Practicing Christian's (We) love for the Church should be apparent from its in-depth and always charitable reasoning about how to approach church leadership with this issue. We do not want to make this issue divisive, but merely get churches to understand the freedom and power they have in the Bible and Constitution when they don't voluntarily give away their rights and sovereignty.

The whole book is filled with revelations and implications that need to be thought about and considered. So, I highly recommend this book to anyone, who like myself, is perplexed and disheartened about what is happening in our country. And to anyone who wonders why the church seems as anemic and pitiful in its role as salt - a preservative, a healing agent, and an irritant. It seems clear, that turning this country from corruption, from decadence, from tyranny onto the long road back to freedom starts with someone like yourself, humbly and respectfully bringing to the attention of even just one incorporated church that they have chosen a second master whom they must obey - instead of Jesus. If they will but give up this second master, and his perks, they will find great freedom to bring glory to God. You won't get a better education and practical application for this task than by reading Greenwood's book: The CORPORATION SOLE Freeing America's Pulpits from the Restrictive 501c3 Laws for Churches.

---Connie Tripp, Director and Overseer of the 24/6 Rehab Training Center in Fairfield, California.

About Overseer Joshua Kenny-Greenwood

Joshua and his wife Mandy have been in ministry for 13 years. Years ago they both founded The Empowerment Center Church here in Sun River, Oregon with the vision of FREEING The Church from todays restrictive 501c3 laws and helping to RAISE UP the next generation of leaders for the Body of Christ. As of 2014, Joshua has helped teach over 26,000+ Pastors, he has personally helped establish thousands of Churches here in North America and he also enjoys the distinction of having written & published the first book in American history related to the Corporation Sole and modern day tax law. Joshua also enjoys being able to preach daily to The Empowerment Center's 30,000+ fans and listeners on Facebook. When he is not ministering to Pastors, Joshua enjoys spending time with his wife and his awesome three Children (Jacob Alexander, Justin David and Faith Victoria).

Church 14 Points
(p.

CPSIA information can be obtained
at www.ICGtesting.com
Printed in the USA
LVHW090248100419
613611LV00001B/52/P